THE DAY OF THE PICNIC

Russell Davis

BROADWAY PLAY PUBLISHING INC
New York
www.broadwayplaypublishing.com
info@broadwayplaypublishing.com

Cover art by Kat O'Brien
First printing: February 2014
I S B N: 978-0-88145-589-2
Book design: Marie Donovan
Page make-up: Adobe Indesign
Typeface: Palatino
Printed and bound in the U S A

There were readings and development work of THE DAY OF THE PICNIC at Playwrights Theatre of New Jersey, PlayPenn, New Dramatists & the O'Neill Center's National Playwrights Conference.

A previous version THE DAY OF THE PICNIC was produced by Yale Repertory Theatre, New Haven, from 16 January-25 February, 1984. The cast and creative contributors were:

BETSY FULLBRIGHT	Margaret Hilton
JULIUS NKUMBI	James Earl Jones
DENISE JONES	Theresa Merritt
DINKO TASOVAC	Ron Faber
NANI NAM YUM	Lori Tan Chinn
STANLEY KRONENBERG	Carl Low
STAFF	Patricia Clarkson
Director	Tony Giordano
Set	Peter Maradudin
Costumes	Charles Henry McClennahan
Lights	Tom Roscher
Sound	Robert Chase
Stage manager	Sue Ruocco
Dramaturg	Gitta Honegger
Assistant director	Terrence J Witter

THE DAY OF THE PICNIC was subsequently produced by People's Light & Theatre Company, Malvern, PA, from 28 January-15 February 2009. The cast and creative contributors were:

BETSY FULLBRIGHT	Carla Belver
JULIUS NKUMBI	Michael Rogers
DENISE JONES	Brenda Thomas
DINKO TASOVAC	Graham Smith
UDAYA (DAWN) KUMARI SASTRI	Nalini Sharma
ELIJAH	Graham Smith
SECOND (or DEUTERO) ISAIAH	Alda Cortese
MARY MAGDALENE	Nalini Sharma
COOKIE BRAULT	Alda Cortese

Director	Abigail Adams
Set	Matt Saunders
Costumes	Marla J Jurglanis
Lights	Dennis Parichy
Sound	Christopher Colucci
Video design	Jorge Cousineau
Stage manager	Pat G Sabato
Dramaturg	Elizabeth Pool
Dialect coach	Lynne Innerst
Ass't director/choreographer	Samantha Bellomo

CHARACTERS

BETSY FULLBRIGHT, *a retired person*
JULIUS NKUMBI, *a silent black man in a wheelchair*
DENISE JONES, *a retired person, African-American*
DINKO TASOVAC, *recently arrived from another institution*
UDAYA (DAWN) KUMARI SASTRI, *who comes to visit* BETSY
FULLBRIGHT
ELIJAH, *a Hebrew prophet*
SECOND (OR DEUTERO) ISAIAH, *a prophetess*
MARY MAGDALENE, *an early Christian*
COOKIE BRAULT, *another retired person*
a member of the retirement home STAFF

Note: a cast of six is adequate, as the roles of ELIJAH,
DEUTERO-ISAIAH, MARY MAGDALENE *and retirement
home* STAFF *can all be doubled.*

SETTING

The day room in a retirement home in the United States.

There are several tables, chairs, a bookcase and television set. On one wall is a muzak speaker. On another wall is a framed picture, or print, of a mountain top.

A large sliding glass door is upstage with a patio outside.

On one side of the stage is the entrance from the women's hall. On the other side is the entrance from the men's hall. Downstage to one side is the entrance from the main reception area.

Time: September. Not too long ago.

ACT ONE

(The sound of muzak)

(BETSY FULLBRIGHT sits at a table. She reads.)

(JULIUS sits at another table in his wheelchair. He watches BETSY. He holds a cassette player on his lap.)

(It is morning.)

(The muzak stops.)

(Pause)

A VOICE: *(Offstage)* Yoo hoo!

(BETSY looks up.)

(DENISE JONES enters from the women's hallway. She wears a shower cap and bathrobe.)

(BETSY and DENISE regard each other.)

DENISE: Did you do that?

BETSY: Excuse me?

DENISE: Did you say yoo hoo?

BETSY: I did not.

DENISE: Sounded like you. Just now.

BETSY: No, I haven't said a thing.

DENISE: Somebody is saying yoo hoo.

BETSY: Not in here.

DENISE: Nobody in here?

BETSY: Perhaps there's a person on the lawn.

DENISE: Calling out yoo hoo?

BETSY: Sounds it, yes.

(DENISE *goes to the patio door upstage. She opens it. She looks out.*)

DENISE: I see no one. Out here on the lawn.

BETSY: How about the road?

DENISE: What road?

BETSY: Down by the road. The highway.

DENISE: Can't see.

BETSY: Behind the hedges, don't you suppose?

DENISE: I don't know. I heard it before.

BETSY: You have?

DENISE: I did, yeah. This yoo hoo.

BETSY: I have too.

DENISE: You heard it?

BETSY: Oh, yes. Several times.

DENISE: Hm. Who could be doing that? Calling yoo hoo. (*She closes the patio door.*)

(BETSY *picks up her book. She reads.*)

DENISE: Hot.

BETSY: Hm?

DENISE: Hot out there. Way too hot for September.

BETSY: Much too hot, yes. Let's hope the air conditioning holds.

DENISE: Uh huh. Feels like Africa out there. The desert. (*She looks at the thermostat on the wall. She regards* BETSY.) This seem curious to you? This yoo hoo?

BETSY: Somewhat.

DENISE: It seem awful curious to me.

BETSY: I'm sure there's a reason.

DENISE: Uh huh. How many times you heard it?

BETSY: *(Trying to read)* Excuse me?

DENISE: The yoo hoo. I heard it seven times.

BETSY: Seven, you say?

DENISE: Uh huh. How about you?

BETSY: I hadn't counted, no.

DENISE: The first time I was asleep minding my business. Blasted me right out of bed like a trumpet, the first yoo hoo.

BETSY: I'm sorry.

DENISE: My ears was ringing like the walls of Jericho. The next time it just whispered. Like a tip toe. I could barely notice.

BETSY: I'm sure it's just a stranger, that's all.

DENISE: Hm?

BETSY: As I said. Some silly passer-by. Making these sounds.

DENISE: There's no stranger out there, I told you. No one to see.

BETSY: Well, someone waiting, then. For a bus, I suppose. The bus is late. So now they're hollering.

DENISE: For what bus?

BETSY: Out there there's a bus, I believe. A stop for a bus, yes. Across our lawn. The other side of the hedge. Where we can't see.

DENISE: Nobody hollers yoo hoo like that for a bus.

BETSY: People do very strange things these days.

DENISE: I don't think there's even a bus stop.

BETSY: What, at the end of our lawn?

DENISE: It's just highway down there.

BETSY: Well, some other reason, then. Like a breakdown. Some car perhaps has had a breakdown.

DENISE: Nobody hollers yoo hoo like that over a breakdown.

BETSY: Well. I suppose it must be the heat.

DENISE: Yeah?

BETSY: The heat, yes. Must be bothering some stranger out there. Some poor person out for a stroll. At the end of our lawn. *(She returns to reading.)*

*(*DENISE *sits down at the table across from* BETSY. *She ponders.)*

DENISE: I don't know. What's curious to me is the voice of this stranger. The voice that's making the yoo hoo out there.

BETSY: Hm?

DENISE: The yoo hoo. Cause this time it sounded like you. Could be you out there.

BETSY: It wasn't, no.

DENISE: Last time it sounded like me. Did you notice?

BETSY: Excuse me?

DENISE: The yoo hoo sounded like me. Like my own voice.

BETSY: Ah.

DENISE: Like my voice left my body and spoke to me. Spooky.

BETSY: *(Reading)* What was that?

DENISE: It was spooky. I was in the shower, as a matter of fact. That time it yoo hooed. With soap on half my body.

A VOICE: (*Offstage*) Yoo hoo!

(DENISE *gets up from the table.*)

(BETSY *looks up.*)

DENISE: Sounded like me again. Didn't it sound like me?

BETSY: I'm sure it's just the lawn.

DENISE: The lawn?

BETSY: Well, yes. It's hot out there. Humid. You said so yourself.

DENISE: There's nobody on the lawn.

BETSY: Well, but something's out there.

DENISE: Don't give me no lawn. That sounded like me. Even felt like me. Like somebody snuck up and picked my mind. Made it yoo hoo out there.

BETSY: But we both know it wasn't you.

DENISE: We know that?

BETSY: Yes. You're right here with me. Talking.

DENISE: Could still be something in my mind.

BETSY: What could?

DENISE: That took a yoo hoo out there.

BETSY: That's silly. Nonsense. There's nothing in our conversation, no moment at all, where one of us stood up, or went outside, and shouted a yoo hoo. And the other didn't see, I assure you. So whatever's going on, whatever yoo hoo, it's out there. On its own.

(DENISE *regards the patio doubtfully.*)

DENISE: I don't know. Feels spooky all over again.

BETSY: It's probably just the sound, that's all. Sound waves. The heat affects the sound of things.

DENISE: What sound?

BETSY: The sounds. The general sound. The leaves, perhaps. The birds. They sound different.

DENISE: Yeah. Yeah, this is a lot of heat for September.

BETSY: One tends to hear things.

DENISE: Could be little mirages. Sound mirages.

BETSY: Precisely.

DENISE: Maybe a leaf gets blown a little, squeaks maybe, maybe somebody has squeaky shoes passing by on our lawn, or by the highway, and this, because of the weather outside, combined also with what you're thinking, what you remember, can cause a yoo hoo to be heard.
It's not so frequent anyway.
(She goes to the television. She turns it on.)

(BETSY returns to her book.)

DENISE: Did you have breakfast?

BETSY: Hm?

DENISE: There was breakfast?

BETSY: No, actually. I woke up late. For some reason.

DENISE: I did too. I missed my breakfast.

BETSY: Yes. I wasn't well.

DENISE: I never miss breakfast. I must have ate something last night to make me miss my breakfast like this. And the picnic. I was looking forward too on being on a picnic. I never miss a picnic outing like this.
(Pause)
Something's wrong with the television.

BETSY: Hm?

DENISE: There's no sound. I can get no sound.

BETSY: Well.

DENISE: I want sound. It's dead, the sound. Furthermore, I can't seem to change the channel. It's stuck to one channel. *(She kicks the television.)*

BETSY: Careful. Perhaps you should inform the staff.

DENISE: No sound. What are the first two things I do everyday? Before breakfast.

BETSY: I don't know.

DENISE: I take a shower and I watch the news.

BETSY Of course.

DENISE: Everyday. However this morning I hear a yoo hoo in the shower, so one part of me didn't get soaped. And now this television, it has no sound. As a matter of fact, it's not even shutting off. *(Fiddling with the knobs)* I can't make it go off. *(Pause. She regards the screen.)*

DENISE: Look at that. Look at all these foreign people. They're burning flags. In Guatemala.

BETSY: Flags, you say?

DENISE: There's a subtitle says Guatemala.

BETSY: Well, Guatemala.

DENISE: Now they've gone to Saudi Arabia.

BETSY: What, to burn flags?

DENISE: Uh huh. That's what the subtitle says.

BETSY: Must be a riot.

DENISE: American flags.

BETSY: Oh, dear.

DENISE: Hm. Egypt too. They're ripping down a flag in Egypt.

BETSY: Our flag?

DENISE: Looks British. Or French.

BETSY: Ah. Perhaps the Suez. *(She gets up from the table. She joins* DENISE *at the television.)* My goodness.

DENISE: Uh huh. Yep.

BETSY: Goodness. Look at all those bonfires. Some television programmer is obviously trying to make some sort of point.

DENISE: What point?

BETSY: Well, a point, I'm sure, about western society.

DENISE: There's no point.

BETSY: Of course, there's a point. Look at our flags.

DENISE: Then how come there's no sound? If they had a point, there'd be sound.

BETSY: I'm sure they intended to have sound.

DENISE: Nope. No sound.

BETSY: But you just said it's broken. The television.

DENISE: We don't know if it's broken.

BETSY: Well, but if there's no sound.

DENISE: This could be on purpose.

BETSY: What, not changing channels like you said, that's on purpose?

(Pause. BETSY *and* DENISE *look in astonishment at the television.)*

BETSY: That man is defecating.

DENISE: Uh huh. I know.

BETSY: That masked man is defecating right there on the television.

DENISE: The Philippines, uh huh.

BETSY: Right on the American flag.

DENISE: Pakistan.

BETSY: What?

DENISE: Going to the bathroom in Pakistan too.

BETSY: These masked men are defecating on our television.

DENISE: Uh huh. It's awful.

BETSY: This is astounding.

DENISE: That's right. Astounding. How can they hog our channels like this? Who's telling these foreign people to squat like this on our channels?

BETSY: We must turn this thing off.

DENISE: It don't turn off.

BETSY: How can I turn this off?

DENISE: The turn off button is broken.

BETSY: Well, what about the plug?

DENISE: I don't know. This is some program.

(BETSY *pulls the plug out of the wall.*)

(*Pause.* BETSY *and* DENISE *look at the empty screen.*)

BETSY: There. They're gone.

DENISE: Uh huh.

BETSY: Somebody has obviously taken over the local television station, don't you think?

DENISE: They took it over?

BETSY: Yes. How else could they transmit those pictures?

DENISE: Who took it over?

BETSY: Well, I don't know. Obviously some lunatic. With a gun. A lunatic has obviously decided he can do in this country what they do in other countries. Chile, for example. Colombia. Serbia. Where they take over television stations. Hold guns to people's heads. Force them to do things. Make announcements. We have a lunatic on the loose, some barmy person out there in the neighborhood who thinks there's some sort of revolution going on, some upheaval we should have.

A VOICE: *(Offstage)* Yoo hoo!

(Pause)

DENISE: Sounded like you.

BETSY: What did?

DENISE: That yoo hoo.

BETSY: That wasn't my yoo hoo.

DENISE: Yeah. Sounded just like you.

BETSY: It didn't at all.

DENISE: You can't tell your own voice?

BETSY: I know how I sound.

DENISE: That didn't feel like somebody picked your mind?

BETSY: Did what?

DENISE: Picked a yoo hoo from your mind. Made it holler out there?

BETSY: Not at all. That wasn't at all like my yoo hoo out there. *(She goes back to her table. She sits.)*

DENISE: Hm. I think you should admit, Betsy Fullbright. To your own yoo hoo out there. Just like I admit to mine.

BETSY: There's nothing out there, Denise Jones, I assure you. For me to admit to.
(She opens her book. She reads.)

(DENISE puts the television plug back in. She fiddles with the knobs. It doesn't turn on. She fiddles some more.)

BETSY: *(Distracted, looking up)* Perhaps you should change out of your shower cap. Must be time, don't you think?

DENISE: This cap?

BETSY: Yes. You're done with your shower, I take it.

DENISE: What does my shower cap have to do with a yoo hoo? Or the television?

BETSY: Nothing. You look silly.

DENISE: I want to know the connection.

BETSY: I don't see any connection.

DENISE: Hm. Sounds to me like you could calm down, Betsy Fullbright.

BETSY: I'm calm. Perfectly so. Where did you get the idea I wasn't calm?

DENISE: Talking about lunatics taking over the television station is calm?

BETSY: You're the one who kicked it. That's probably what finally did it.

DENISE: Well, I'm not going back to my room. To change clothes. Not till they clear up some matters here. Fix things up. I'm not getting back into that shower.

BETSY: I thought you took a shower.

DENISE: I took half a shower. I heard a yoo hoo, I told you.

BETSY: Very well.

DENISE: So I'm sticking here.

(BETSY reads.)

(DENISE regards JULIUS, who sits silently.)

DENISE: Probably we should all stick here. Keep to the dayroom, I think. Till this yoo hoo passes.

(DENISE *takes a hold of* JULIUS's *wheelchair and wheels him to the table where* BETSY *is sitting.* DENISE *sits down herself.*)

(JULIUS *stares at* BETSY.)

DENISE: Furthermore. I can find no staff to complain to.

BETSY: There's a picnic.

DENISE: There's still supposed to be staff.

BETSY: This man shouldn't be sitting here, Denise. This is my table.

DENISE: He can sit.

BETSY: He'll play something. He'll play music. On that tape recorder.

DENISE: You don't like music?

BETSY: He's staring. Why is this man staring?

DENISE: I guess he's new.

BETSY: Well, I know.

DENISE: His name is Julius Nkumbi. The nurse told me last night. We're television buddies now.

BETSY: Well, I'm reading, do you mind?

DENISE: The television's broke.

BETSY: I'm sorry about your television.

DENISE: So you can read to us.

BETSY: Pardon?

DENISE: (*Looking at cover of* BETSY's *book*) *A Narrative of the Captivity & Restoration of Daniel Bunting.*

BETSY: Do you mind?

DENISE: Who's Daniel Bunting?

BETSY: He was captured. By the Bugandans.

DENISE: Who?

BETSY: A dangerous people, once upon a time, in Africa.

DENISE: Oh? Read it to us.

BETSY: You wouldn't like it.

DENISE: Why not?

BETSY: The hero is an Anglo-Saxon.

DENISE: I like Anglo-Saxons. Do the Bugandans kill this Anglo-Saxon?

BETSY: Well, no, they capture.

DENISE: Just capture?

BETSY: Denise Jones, this man is staring at me.

DENISE: Nkumbi?

BETSY: Why is this man so persistent in his staring?

DENISE: Maybe his eyes are stuck.

BETSY: No, he's staring on purpose.

DENISE: I don't know, they look stuck to me. Julius Nkumbi.

BETSY: Yes. Make him stop.

DENISE: Julius Nkumbi. Put down your eyes. Go on. Put them down.

(JULIUS *shuts his eyes.*)

DENISE: That's better. He just forgets himself, that's all. If he stares.

BETSY: Does he speak?

DENISE: No. They told me he doesn't.

BETSY: The staff?

DENISE: Last night, yeah. They said, Denise Jones, this man doesn't speak. He has no vocal chords now. Let him watch television with you.

BETSY: Ah.

DENISE: But he sure looks like he's thinking.

BETSY: Exactly. He's a distraction.

DENISE: So does he escape?

BETSY: Excuse me?

DENISE: The Anglo-Saxon. Daniel Bunting. Does he escape the Bugandans?

BETSY: He does, yes. Eventually.

DENISE: With his whole body?

BETSY: Pardon?

DENISE: He has both hands? Both ears and feet?

BETSY: Well, yes, he suffers considerably. But nothing actually gets amputated. As far as I know.

DENISE: Uh huh.

BETSY: I believe one eye goes blind. Some loss of hearing. But I believe these might be restored again. Once he returns to civilization.

DENISE: You read this before?

BETSY: Well, yes, it's all rather standard. It's the genre.

DENISE: The what?

BETSY: There are many novels of this genre. A certain literature where an Anglo-Saxon is captured by a primitive people of some sort. These novels always end with the Anglo-Saxon returning to his own kind with a sense of letdown. As if his life now feels tame, or dispirited. The old boundaries, our little enclosures, make no sense. He feels a restlessness he can no longer contain. Probably similar to what Lawrence of Arabia felt when he came home to England and rammed his motorcycle into a tree. Or Glubb Pasha when King Hussein threw him out of Jordan.

Most of these novels were being written, they were very popular, back in the days when the world was still being colonized.

A VOICE: *(Offstage)* Yoo hoo!

(Pause)

DENISE: That came from the hall. Down there.

BETSY: The women's hall?

DENISE: Yeah. The yoo hoo's left the lawn, I think.

BETSY: Who would shout yoo hoo like that down our hall?

A VOICE: *(Offstage)* Yoo hoo!

(Pause)

DENISE: Sounds like your friend.

BETSY: What friend?

DENISE: The one who visited last week. She calls you Auntie.

BETSY: I'm not an auntie.

DENISE: You don't have a niece, or grand-niece?

BETSY: Oh. You must mean that distant in-law. On my husband's side. Adopted, I think, from some other land.

DENISE: Well, she calls you Auntie.

BETSY: She's just taken to visiting for now, that's all.

A VOICE: *(Offstage)* Yoo hoo!

(Pause)

DENISE: That's definitely your friend. Down our hall. The one who calls you Auntie.

BETSY: Perhaps it's been her all along.

DENISE: Doing the yoo hoos?

BETSY: Perhaps, yes.

DENISE: Can she do different voices? Is she spooky?
Like this yoo hoo?

BETSY: Well, I don't know. She does seem to get silly
sometimes.

DENISE: Hm. Maybe I should check and see. Catch
who's at the bottom to this. We should split up.

BETSY: You're going to walk down there?

DENISE: Uh huh. You listen in case there's still a yoo
hoo in here.

BETSY: I thought you said we should stick together.

DENISE: I'll come back soon. We can stick together then.
(She exits down the women's hallway.)

(BETSY regards her book.)

*(JULIUS, in his wheelchair, slowly raises a finger. He presses
the REWIND button on the cassette player in his lap. He
presses the STOP button. He presses the PLAY button.)*

(The sound of static)

(The meow of a large cat)

(JULIUS presses the STOP button. He closes his eyes.)

(BETSY stares at him.)

*(Enter DINKO TASOVAC from the men's hallway. He
creeps along the walls of the day room toward the women's
hallway.)*

(BETSY watches.)

BETSY: Why are you tiptoeing?

DINKO: Excuse me?

BETSY: I'm very curious.

DINKO: Tiptoeing?

BETSY: Yes. You were tiptoeing.

DINKO: Oh. They didn't tell you? I thought maybe they had.

BETSY: Tell me what?

DINKO: There's been some trouble.

BETSY: Oh?

DINKO: Did you notice somebody walking around causing some trouble?

BETSY: No, I hadn't. What sort of trouble?

DINKO: Sometimes it's outside, sometimes it's inside. It's a lot of trouble, this trouble.

BETSY: I see.

DINKO: Anyway. They said we should keep quiet around here. Be on our tiptoes. Because of the trouble. *(He continues to tiptoe toward the women's hallway.)*

(BETSY stands. She watches.)

BETSY: You can't do that, by the way.

DINKO: Hm? Do what?

BETSY: Sneak like that, I think, toward the ladies' hall.

DINKO: Who, me? The ladies' hall?

BETSY: Yes, it's not allowed.

DINKO: But I'm looking for this trouble.

BETSY: What trouble?

DINKO: I'm not sure I'm so much at liberty to say.

BETSY: What, to tell trouble?

DINKO: *(Whispering)* Yeah, what should keep us quiet. Very deep, this trouble. I'm amazed you did not know. What they say now.

BETSY: What's this whispering for?

DINKO: Oh. Sorry. *(Still whispering)* I said, What they say now. About Moses.

BETSY: Moses?

DINKO: Uh huh. Plenty of big trouble up ahead. For Moses.

BETSY: Really?

DINKO: Oh, yeh. I thought you would have heard.

BETSY: I'm sorry. What is it I'm supposed to have heard?

DINKO: Just some troublemakers, I'm sure. Archaeologists, you know. Ancient historians, particle physicists, the carbon-14 daters.

BETSY: Yes?

DINKO: These people who complain. About the seven days to creation.

BETSY: Oh?

DINKO: They complain too, this is not the word of God, all this Bible. It's redacted.

BETSY: Redacted?

DINKO: Yeh. You didn't hear of the Great Redactor?

BETSY: No, I haven't.

DINKO: He's called now, I think, the Deuteronomistic Historian.

BETSY: Deuteronomy, what?

DINKO: *(Slowly)* Deuteronomistic Historian. Probably there are more than one of these Deuteronomistic Historians. Probably a whole gang is responsible. Excuse me. I have a very busy schedule now. *(He continues his tiptoe across the room.)*

BETSY: You're not supposed to go down there. The women's hall.

DINKO: I'm looking for the trouble I mentioned.

BETSY: What, this gang of yours?

DINKO: A gang?

BETSY: This gang, you just said, that's causing trouble for Moses.

DINKO: It's not my gang.

BETSY: Well, I'm sure they went the other way.

DINKO: I looked the other way.

BETSY: You should go to your room, I think.

DINKO: *(Suspicious)* What's in my room?

BETSY: You could lie down. Take a rest.

DINKO: No, then the trouble's gonna strike. It likes when I'm sleeping.

BETSY: You're the man, aren't you, who always asleep? Right here in the day room?

DINKO: That's cause I'm busy at night.

BETSY: All day, you just eat and sleep.

DINKO: I got to rest sometime.

BETSY: What is your name?

DINKO: Dinko Tasovac.

BETSY: Ah, yes.

DINKO: Tasovac. You heard of me?

BETSY: Why aren't you at the picnic?

DINKO: I told them I was sick.

BETSY: You don't like picnics?

DINKO: I can't be seen in public with a nursing house.

BETSY: Retirement, actually.

DINKO: I'm on the track anyway of this trouble.

BETSY: What makes you think the trouble's down there? Down this particular ladies' hall?

DINKO: I heard a yoo hoo.

BETSY: Oh?

DINKO: This yoo hoo keeps changing its voice.

BETSY: It does, yes.

DINKO: One time the yoo hoo was even like me. Like I was talking to myself. It's very tricky, this trouble.

BETSY: Well.

DINKO: What's your name, please, you told me, but I forgot.

BETSY: I never told you. You're always asleep.

DINKO: *(Trying to remember)* I got a lousy memory.

BETSY: Betsy Fullbright.

DINKO: Yeah, Fullbright, excuse me now. I got to find what's making this trouble.

(BETSY *steps between* DINKO *and the entrance of the women's hallway.)*

BETSY: You can't go down there. I told you.

DINKO: Sssh. I'm gonna knock the yoo hoo out of it.

BETSY: I will not sssh.

DINKO: It's been nice to talk. *(He slips past* BETSY. *He exits into the hallway.)*

(BETSY *looks down the hall after him.)*

BETSY: Denise Jones! Denise Jones, there's a strange man tiptoeing down our hallway! The man they transferred, I believe, from that institution. The institution across town, remember? He's coming down the hallway. Right now.
Denise?

A VOICE: *(Offstage)* Yoo hoo!

(BETSY turns. She regards the opposite hallway. She crosses the day room. She stands at the entrance to the men's hallway.)

BETSY: *(Down the hallway)* Hello?
Hello? Is there someone down there?
Did someone call out just now?

(No response)

(BETSY turns back to the day room.)

(JULIUS is staring at her.)

(BETSY frowns. She steps forward and takes the handles of his wheelchair. She wheels him toward the patio. She leaves him upstage, looking out the sliding glass door. She comes back to her table. She sits. She opens her book. She reads.)

(JULIUS slowly turns his wheelchair around. He raises a finger and presses the PLAY button on his cassette.)

(The sound of static.)

(The meow of a large cat. The meow turns into a scream. Then a death rattle.)

(Silence)

(JULIUS presses the STOP button.)

(BETSY stares at him.)

(DENISE enters from the women's hallway.)

BETSY: Did you hear that?

DENISE: What?

BETSY: The cat? Did you hear what he has?

DENISE: What cat?

BETSY: He's got a cat, or something, on his cassette.
Someone kills a cat. Like a sacrifice. It's recorded.

DENISE: Really?

BETSY: Now why would someone record that? The death of a cat. What could prompt someone?

DENISE: Mister Nkumbi, do you have a cat in there? Somebody's dead cat?

BETSY: He's not speaking.

DENISE: I know he don't speak, but he can show. Mister Nkumbi, you want to show us again the cat?

BETSY: I'd rather he not, actually.

(JULIUS *slowly raises a finger.*)

DENISE: He's going to show. He's going to play us his cat.

(JULIUS *presses the REWIND button. He presses the PLAY button. Pause. Nothing. He presses the STOP button.*)

DENISE: I guess not. It's nothing now.
Thank you anyway, Mister Nkumbi.

BETSY: Well, it's just horrible.

DENISE: *(Wheeling* JULIUS *toward the television)* I guess it's private.

(BETSY *sits at her table.*)

(DENISE *fiddles with the television knobs. It doesn't turn on.*)

BETSY: Did you happen to find what you were looking for? Down our hall?

DENISE: Nope. I can find nobody down there.

BETSY: You didn't see that man?

DENISE: *(Thumping television)* What man?

BETSY: The one called Toecoe, I think. Taco. Dinko Taco.

DENISE: The one who's always sleeping?

BETSY: That one, yes. He was tiptoeing down our hall.

DENISE: I didn't see him.

BETSY: Well, I shouted to you about him. He came in here mentioning a troublemaker. Then headed off down our hall.

DENISE: A troublemaker, uh huh?

BETSY: Someone, yes, who says yoo hoo.

DENISE: Ah.

BETSY: He mentioned also a gang.

DENISE: A gang, yeah?

BETSY: Some folks, yes. Looking to cause trouble for Moses.

DENISE: There's a gang out there against Moses?

BETSY: Well, I couldn't follow exactly. He mentioned some kind of historian. Some people who protest, I assume. In some way or other, the veracity of our Bible.

DENISE: Oh, boy.

BETSY: Anyway, I do think Mister Dinko actually comes from that institution. The one across town, you know.

DENISE: The mental institution?

BETSY: I believe so, yes.

(A young woman, UDAYA [DAWN] KUMARI SASTRI, appears at the downstage entrance from the main reception area.)

UDAYA DAWN: Auntie? Hello? Auntie Fullbright?

(BETSY and DENISE turn. They regard UDAYA DAWN.)

UDAYA DAWN: Hello, Auntie. I have come again to visit. Do you happen to know where there are the staff?

BETSY: The staff?

DENISE: Didn't I say they left no staff?

UDAYA DAWN: Yes. I wanted to sign in for my visit.

BETSY: There has to be staff.

DENISE: Nope. They all went to the picnic.

BETSY: That's not possible. Perhaps they're all upstairs.

UDAYA DAWN: Upstairs, you think?

BETSY: Yes, would you mind, please, going upstairs and getting us some staff?

UDAYA DAWN: Of course, Auntie. I will find these staff for you.

DENISE: *(Whispering to* BETSY*)* What's her name?

BETSY: Pardon?

DENISE: *(Whispering to* BETSY*)* What's the name to your friend?

UDAYA DAWN: *(To* DENISE*)* Oh, I can help you. My name is Udaya. But please you can call me Dawn.

DENISE: Dawn, huh?

UDAYA DAWN: How do you do, yes?

DENISE: Dawn, yeah, did you happen to hear some calling out? Like a yoo hoo?

UDAYA DAWN: A yoo hoo?

DENISE: Yeah, different voices yelling yoo hoo?

UDAYA DAWN: Well, yes, I believe so. Just as I parked my car, I heard someone call this. And then too as I entered your building.

DENISE: Uh huh. And who do you think is making these yoo hoos?

UDAYA DAWN: Oh, several people, I suppose.

DENISE: Uh huh. Did one of them sound like you? Did you hear yourself maybe make a yoo hoo?

UDAYA DAWN: Oh, yes. But I was not speaking. So I paid it no mind.

BETSY: That's all right, Dawn, dear. You should go upstairs now and bring us down the staff.

UDAYA DAWN: Of course, Auntie. I will find for you some staff. *(She exits downstage back out into the reception area.)*

(Pause)

DENISE: Well, that's good.

BETSY: Yes.

DENISE: There's someone here to look for the staff.

BETSY: I think so too.

DENISE: She seems very nice. She obeys so good, this grand-niece, or distant in-law of yours.

BETSY: Yes, she goes to school around here, evidently. Some program. She decided to look me up.

DENISE: Uh huh.

BETSY: Imagine. Someone on Kenneth's side of the family like this. Looking me up.

DENISE: Kenneth?

BETSY: Well, yes, my husband. Kenneth Fullbright. We lived abroad, you know. Africa, in fact.

DENISE: You lived in Africa?

BETSY: Oh, yes. All our married life. Kenya, mostly. That's why I have no idea who this Dawn dear is.

DENISE: I didn't know that.

BETSY: Well, it's not the sort of thing one would talk about, I suppose. But my husband did do many wonderful works, you know, over there in Africa. And I was there all along. To assist and support him.

DENISE: Uh huh. Is Kenya where Nairobi is?

BETSY: That's right.

DENISE: Yeah. I heard about that somewhere, maybe on television. Kenya was like a British Vietnam, yeah?

BETSY: No, of course not. You must be thinking of the Boer War, dear.

DENISE: Uh huh. I heard somewhere it was Kenya too.

BETSY: Well, there were disturbances, sure. Skirmishes. I remember word of skirmishes. Kenneth would tell me.

DENISE: Yeah, I read somewhere too how memory can play tricks. On certain old people.

BETSY: Tricks on what old people?

DENISE: Old white people, like the British. Who lived once in Kenya.

BETSY: But I'm not British.

DENISE: Oh. Well, that means you must be okay.

BETSY: Yes, my husband. He was British.

DENISE: Uh huh. And how come you're here?

BETSY: Well, but my husband died. They put me here. The church organization Kenneth always worked for. They're supposed to care for us, you know, as we get on. As we lose our husbands. Our various loved ones.

DENISE: Yeah.

(Pause. She sits with BETSY *at the table.)*

BETSY: Still. It does seem rather hot. Doesn't it seem hot to you today?

DENISE: It does, yeah.

BETSY: As hot as I ever remember it in Kenya.

DENISE: Hot, yeah. Phew. Like a heat wave in here.

BETSY: Do you suppose our air conditioning has failed?

DENISE: Yeah, seems so.

BETSY: Or could it be that the heat has gone on?

DENISE: Yeah. Could be that boiler downstairs.

BETSY: Yes, I suppose it could.

(BETSY *and* DENISE *fan themselves at the table.*)

DENISE: Don't it seem extra quiet too, you think? This morning?

BETSY: Quiet? Well, yes, I think so.

DENISE: Like there's no staff?

BETSY: There's staff. They're upstairs.

DENISE: We don't know that.

BETSY: Yes, we do. We sent that Dawn person after them.

DENISE: Something's making this place quiet then.

BETSY: Yes, very quiet.

DENISE: Like a needle could drop. Feels like something around here, I think, could be building up. To call out another yoo hoo.
What do you think?

BETSY: Well, I don't know.

(BETSY *and* DENISE *regard the day room.*)

BETSY: Perhaps it's just the television, remember. It's broken.

DENISE: That's right. There's usually all sorts of television sound in here.

BETSY: And then there's Cookie Brault too. She's at the picnic.

DENISE: Yeah?

BETSY: Well, it's always much quieter when Cookie Brault is absent.

DENISE: You know, as a matter of fact, I can't remember Cookie Brault practicing her reveille this morning.

BETSY: Yes, I think you're right. I can't remember either.

DENISE: That do annoy me.

BETSY: And how about the National Anthem?

DENISE: Yeah, I don't remember hearing the National Anthem on her speakers down the hall.

BETSY: Hm. I wonder if the flag's up, do you think? Is it possible Cookie Brault didn't put her flag up?

(BETSY *and* DENISE *go upstage to the patio door. They look out.*)

BETSY: It's not up.

DENISE: Cookie Brault must have messed up.

BETSY: I wonder what that could mean.

DENISE: Maybe the wind took it, that's all.

BETSY: You suppose?

DENISE: Or the staff. Maybe the staff finally spoke about making such a racket every day.

BETSY: Yes. (*Pause*) Have you missed a picnic before?

DENISE: Nope.

BETSY: I haven't either. I was sick.

DENISE: Oh, yeah?

BETSY: Right after dinner last night.

DENISE: Yeah, I was sick then too.

BETSY: I didn't recover, I don't think, till mid-morning or so.

DENISE: Then it disappeared all of a sudden, right? First time I heard a yoo hoo, it disappeared.

BETSY: Perhaps it was my hot chocolate.

DENISE: Yeah. Yeah, you asked me to taste your chocolate.

BETSY: So I did.

DENISE: It was bad.

BETSY: I thought it tasted funny.

DENISE: Maybe something fell in the cup.

BETSY: What would do that?

DENISE: Some kind of enema, maybe?

BETSY: I can't imagine.

DENISE: Maybe Cookie Brault. Cookie Brault's real fond of messing in other people's chocolate.

BETSY: She wouldn't do that.

DENISE: *(Seeing* JULIUS*)* Uh oh. His eyes is stuck again. He's staring.

BETSY: Mister Numby is?

(JULIUS *stares at* BETSY.*)*

DENISE: Julius Nkumbi. You must stop that staring. It's not right to stare like this in front of people. Go on. Put your eyes down.

(JULIUS *shuts his eyes.)*

DENISE: There. He just forgot himself again, that's all. If he stares.

(BETSY *steps away from the patio door.)*

BETSY: I know what it is. Why this place is so quiet. When was the last time you heard muzak?

DENISE: Muzak?

BETSY: There's always been muzak.

(BETSY *and* DENISE *regard the Muzak speaker on the wall.)*

DENISE: Yeah. Yeah, there's none of that music.

BETSY: That's correct.

DENISE: How could there be no music?

BETSY: Well, we'll have to inform the staff of this as well. When the Dawn person brings them down.

(BETSY *sits down at her table*. DENISE *joins her*.)

DENISE: Feels spooky in here, I think, with no music.

BETSY: Please. You're pushing the table.

DENISE: That's probably even why they have it.

BETSY: Have what?

DENISE: Music. To keep us from feeling spooky. Keep us from hearing the yoo hoo underneath.

BETSY: The what underneath?

DENISE: Lurking beneath everything could be this yoo hoo.

BETSY: I rather think not.

A VOICE: *(Offstage)* Yoo hoo!

(Pause)

DENISE: I told you, didn't I, another yoo hoo was building up?

BETSY: Yes. You did.

DENISE: Did this one sound like Cookie Brault to you?

BETSY: I believe so.

DENISE: You think maybe it *was* Cookie Brault?

BETSY: Well, I don't know.

DENISE: I don't either. I think nothing can be sure with this yoo hoo.

BETSY: Well, we can be sure, anyway, it's just some silliness, that's all.

DENISE: You think so?

BETSY: Oh, yes. I'm sure it will pass.

DENISE: Nope. I wonder now if it could be dead people out there. Some kind of visionary folk.

BETSY: Dead people?

DENISE: Yep, all along. The first yoo hoo I heard. Sounded maybe like my mother. Now I think about it, it's certain.

BETSY: Well, that's silly.

DENISE: You haven't heard, maybe, your husband?

BETSY: Kenneth? Of course not.

DENISE: No yoo hoo ever from him?

BETSY: Never.

DENISE: Then maybe it's just ourselves. We can hear ourselves. We could be dead.

BETSY: Pardon?

DENISE: Dead, yep. Only a yoo hoo is left.

(Pause)

BETSY: Do you normally do this? Jump to conclusions?

DENISE: You have a different explanation?

BETSY: Yes, this certainly doesn't mean I should feel I'm dead.

DENISE: This feels like living to you?

BETSY: Well, yes. Of course, it's living.

DENISE: Uh huh. Somebody shouting yoo hoo could never used to scare me. Make me think some dead spirits is surrounding us out there. Getting ready, I expect, to take us away captive.

BETSY: Captive, you'd say? Spirits?

DENISE: Uh huh. Furthermore, I believe if you hear things, like voices, on a regular basis, what should be

just a yoo hoo, it's not too much longer before you start
seeing things also. Visions even, like trances. Which
can only mean maybe two things.
Either you are blessed indeed. Or you are surely
cursed.

(Pause)

BETSY: Well. I think you're overreacting. In fact, I'm
certain of it.

(Pause)

Let me say what I learned from Kenneth. What he
would suggest. It's important, sometimes, to proceed
as if things were normal. Quite regular.
Like if a horse throws you. It's best to get back on.
There are occasions, when we might feel ourselves
surrounded. By an influence. Some murky thing. It
happens to the best of us. And these murky things,
these yoo hoos, would have us believe there is
something incomprehensible now, or irresistible. What
we can't quite put our finger on.
The important thing is to behave as if nothing
is unusual. Hold the mental fort, you know. Till
reinforcements arrive.
Yes. That's what Kenneth would suggest.
Because at some point, of course, our picnic has to
come back. It'll all return, you know. To normal.
And whatever it is, this yoo hoo will be gone. We
won't need anymore, at all, to keep questioning
ourselves like this.

(Pause)

There are certain minds, Kenneth would say, that
would like to spook us. Cause us to question our logic.
Our civilized acceptance of what is reality.

(Pause)

My husband sometimes went on certain distant
journeys to other interiors. I would be left behind.

And some of the native servants, I became convinced,
would try to spook me. Forks would disappear from
their place in a drawer and reappear somewhere odd.
Embedded, for example, in a wall. Or a fork might
be folded up in a blouse of mine. If I put something
away, such as clothes, or a book, they would be taken
out again as if I had never moved them. All of which I
think was intended to induce a certain disorientation.
A vulnerability. Where nothing I thought made sense.
I was susceptible to some mystery in things. In fact,
helpless to those very forces and superstitions western
civilization has spent the last seven hundred years or
so dispelling. And what is distressing is to find these
fears and primitive rhythms rising again within our
very own walls. For example, modern music. Or those
paintings. It's as if our artistic and intellectual leaders
have come to decide all our work is wrong. The labor
of centuries, the cultivation of good manners, proper
education, is all wrong. Yes. Our artists, Kenneth
would say, our thinkers have all gone savage. They
idealize now the barbarian. What our civilization
conquered. Those primitive beliefs and urges out there
have popped back up again. Behind our own front
lines. In our culture. Our very own children.
There is, after all this time, something else to finally
admit. A hocus pocus to the world.
(*She notices her book. She opens it and holds up a fork.*)
Did you do this?

DENISE: Do what?

BETSY: Take my bookmark? Put this fork instead in my
book?

A VOICE: (*Offstage*) Yoo hoo!

(BETSY *and* DENISE *regard the framed picture, or print, on
the wall. It's tilted, or leaning, to one side.*)

BETSY: I think that was the picture.

DENISE: Yeah. That picture just spoke.

(BETSY *stands. She goes to the picture, putting aside the fork.*)

DENISE: Is there somebody in that picture?

BETSY: No. It's just an empty mountain top.

DENISE: Uh huh.

BETSY: *(Peering at picture)* It says Mount Horeb.

DENISE: Mount Horeb?

BETSY: Yes, Mount Horeb. That's the title.

(DENISE *joins* BETSY. *They regard the picture on the wall.*)

DENISE: How come I never noticed before? I just thought this was some regular mountain top, that's all. Did you know, for example, this is Mount Horeb?

BETSY: No, I hadn't realized. Hadn't actually looked.

DENISE: Uh huh. All the way over there in Sinai, can you imagine? Right here on our wall.

BETSY: Yes.

DENISE: That's very considerate. Giving us a picture like this.

BETSY: Yes, it is.

DENISE: It's comforting. It can comfort us. This picture.

(BETSY *reaches forward. She straightens the picture.*)

DENISE: *(Peering closely)* Looks empty now. No one there.

BETSY: Yes, very empty.

DENISE: I can see no Moses, or Elijah, in this picture.

BETSY: I can't either.

DENISE: And yet someone in this picture, for sure, called out yoo hoo.

THE TELEVISION: Yoo hoo!

(BETSY *and* DENISE *turn. They regard the television.*)

DENISE: That was the television. The television just got back its sound.

BETSY: Yes, it did.

DENISE: *(Approaching television)* Look at that.

BETSY: Yes?

DENISE: It looks like our picnic.

BETSY: Yes. A picnic.

DENISE: What's our picnic doing like this on the television?

BETSY: I don't know.

DENISE: Uh oh. There's Cookie Brault.

BETSY: Yes, at the picnic. With her bugle.

DENISE: Mister Dinko too.

BETSY: I see. Sleeping.

DENISE: And there's all the staff.

BETSY: Lots of staff, yes.

DENISE: That's me.

BETSY: Pardon?

DENISE: I'm there at the picnic too. Eating a hot dog.

BETSY: So you are.

DENISE: And there's you.

BETSY: Me?

DENISE: Yes, you. Who're you waving at?

BETSY: I don't know. I can't tell.

DENISE: What's our picnic doing on the television?

BETSY: I don't know.

DENISE: Must be a rerun.

BETSY: Yes, a replay of an old picnic.

DENISE: How come they rerun our picnic?

BETSY: I don't know.

DENISE: *(Proudly)* Must be a special program.

(UDAYA DAWN appears at the downstage entrance from the reception area.)

UDAYA DAWN: Auntie? Hello? Auntie Fullbright?

(BETSY and DENISE turn. They regard UDAYA DAWN.)

UDAYA DAWN: Hello, Auntie. I have come again to visit. Do you happen to know where there are staff?

BETSY: The staff?

UDAYA DAWN: Yes. I wanted to sign in for my visit.

DENISE: What do you mean, sign in? Didn't we send you just now upstairs for the staff?

UDAYA DAWN: The staff are upstairs?

DENISE: Yeah, you're supposed to get the staff upstairs.

UDAYA DAWN: I'm sorry. I did not know.

DENISE: *(To BETSY)* Maybe her English isn't too good.

UDAYA DAWN: *(To DENISE)* Pardon?

DENISE: Your English.

UDAYA DAWN: My English is fine, thank you. I understand very well you say there are staff upstairs.

DENISE: That's right. This time I'm going with you.

UDAYA DAWN: Pardon?

DENISE: Come along, Miss Dawn. We're going upstairs to get the staff.

UDAYA DAWN: *(To BETSY)* I must go upstairs?

BETSY: Yes, would you mind, please, going upstairs with Denise and getting us some staff?

UDAYA DAWN: Of course, Auntie. We will find these staff for you.

DENISE: You stay here. In case there's another yoo hoo. One of those murky things, like you say.

BETSY: Yes, of course.

(Exit DENISE *and* UDAYA DAWN *downstage.)*

*(*BETSY *regards the television. She turns it off. The television won't turn off. She pulls out the plug. The picnic still remains on the screen. She looks uncomfortably at the television. She regards the fork she put aside earlier. She picks it up.)*

*(*JULIUS *slowly raises a finger. He presses the PLAY button on his cassette.)*

JULIUS NKUMBI: *(*BETSY*'s voice)* Does he speak?

CASSETTE: *(*DENISE*'s voice)* No. they told me he doesn't.

*(*BETSY*'s voice)* The staff?

*(*DENISE*'s voice)* Last night, yeah. They said, Denise Jones, this man doesn't speak. He has no vocal chords now. Let him watch television with you.

*(*BETSY*'s voice)* Ah.

*(*DENISE*'s voice)* But he sure looks like he's thinking.

*(*JULIUS *presses the STOP button.)*

*(*BETSY *stares at* JULIUS. *She abruptly steps upstage and opens the sliding patio door. She takes a hold of his wheelchair and wheels it upstage, out onto the patio. She tosses the fork out after him. She comes back in. She sees the television still on. She wheels the television upstage and out onto the patio. She regards him and the television the other side of the door. She turns back to the room. She sees a second fork embedded in the wall above the bookcase. She*

goes to the bookcase. She pulls the fork out of the wall. She goes back to the sliding patio door and throws the fork out onto the lawn. She closes the door. She takes a hold of the curtains to the side of the door and draws them shut. She returns to her table. She stares.)

(The picture on the wall suddenly tilts again. She goes to it. She straightens it.)

(Enter DINKO from the women's hallway. He creeps along the walls of the day room toward the men's hallway. BETSY watches.)

BETSY: You're tiptoeing again.

DINKO: Excuse me?

BETSY: I said, Tiptoeing.

DINKO: Who, me?

BETSY: Did you find your troublemaker?

DINKO: What troublemaker?

BETSY: You mentioned going down the ladies' hall to locate a trouble-maker. Someone who said yoo hoo.

DINKO: Nah. He's slipped away again, this troublemaker. I'm gonna try again down this hall. *(He continues to tiptoe toward the men's hallway. He stops.)*

(The picture on the wall tilts again. BETSY straightens it.)

DINKO: What's making it dark in here?

BETSY: Dark?

DINKO: Yeh. Very dark.

BETSY: Oh. It must be the curtains. I closed them.

DINKO: You closed the curtains?

BETSY: Yes, I did.

DINKO: Was there somebody lurking who was looking at us from the outside?

BETSY: Well, there might have been. I wasn't sure.

DINKO: That's good. It's good to keep the curtains closed. It's not good to look inside.

(The picture tilts. BETSY straightens it.)

(DINKO tiptoes. He stops.)

DINKO: What's this? Who put a fork in my path?

BETSY: A fork?

DINKO: Yeh, there's a fork on the ground in my path.

BETSY: *(Fussing with the picture)* Well, someone must have dropped it.

DINKO: Not this one.

BETSY: What do you mean, not this one?

DINKO: This fork wasn't here before.

BETSY: How would you know?

DINKO: I always look on the ground before me. Each step I take.

BETSY: Oh?

DINKO: I'm very wary.

BETSY: I see.

DINKO: Besides, can't you see? This fork is sticking up.

BETSY: It's what?

DINKO: Somebody has stabbed with this fork. Into the ground.

(BETSY turns. She regards the fork sticking up in the floor.)

DINKO: I'm gonna have to pull this up out of my way. I can't walk around something like this fork in my path. *(He takes a hold of the fork. He tries to pull it up. It doesn't budge.)* Phew. That's some fork.

(BETSY comes forward. She takes a hold of the fork. She pulls. It lifts easily.)

DINKO: Wow. You must be King Arthur.

BETSY: King Arthur?

DINKO: Yeh. I couldn't budge that fork.

BETSY: Your hands must be slippery, that's all.

DINKO: Nah, I got a good grip on my hands.

BETSY: Well, anyway, here it is. Your fork.

DINKO: Nah, you pulled it from the ground. You're the King Arthur.

BETSY: Stop saying King Arthur.

DINKO: I'm not taking the Excalibur fork from you. *(He continues to tiptoe across the room.)*

*(*BETSY *stands watching, holding the fork. She puts it down on a table.)*

BETSY: Ah. Mister Dinko Taco?

DINKO: My name is Tasovac.

BETSY: Pardon?

DINKO: Dinko Tasovac.

BETSY: Sorry. I won't call you Taco again.

DINKO: It's okay.

BETSY: What did you mean, Mister Dinko, when you mentioned some trouble up ahead? I mean, with Moses?

DINKO: I mentioned trouble up ahead? For Moses?

BETSY: You said something, yes.

DINKO: Hm. I confided like this to you?

BETSY: About Deuteronomy, yes. Some sort of gang, you said.

DINKO: Wow.

BETSY: Pardon?

DINKO: That's pretty confidential. I'm surprised I took you so soon in my confidence. You must be quite a lady. Probably you can cast a hell of a spell.

BETSY: Well, thank you.

DINKO: Excuse me now. I'm pretty busy now on my schedule.

(He continues to tiptoe across the room.)

(BETSY follows.)

BETSY: No, tell me, Mister Dinko. I'd like to know. You mentioned something, I believe, about a Great Redactor.

DINKO: Yeh, he's called now the Deuteronomistic Historian.

BETSY: That's him. I'd like to know a little more, if I could, about this Deuteronomomistical Historian.

DINKO: Deuteronomistic.

BETSY: Pardon?

DINKO: It's not mystical. It's a fact.

BETSY: I'm sorry, I can't quite follow.

DINKO: Excuse me. I'm too busy right now to talk.
(He continues to tiptoe.)

(BETSY steps forward and stands between DINKO and the men's hallway entrance.)

BETSY: You're a transfer, aren't you, Mister Dinko?

DINKO: Who, me?

BETSY: Yes, from the mental hospital across town.

DINKO: Nah. I come from around a coupla towns.

BETSY: The mental patient transfers are younger.

DINKO: Beirut. Budapest. Zagreb. Belgrade.

BETSY: How old are you?

DINKO: Havana. Very old.

BETSY: You don't look more than fifty.

DINKO: You should have seen me when I was fifty.

BETSY: I bet.

DINKO: I was something standing on the streets of Havana. We could have got married, by the way.

BETSY: I don't think so, no.

DINKO: No, really, I know how to handle a lady with a spell.

BETSY: I see.

DINKO: We should talk more often, I think, with the curtains closed like so. I was written up, you know, in the Havana papers with ladies like you.

BETSY: Please. Mister Dinko, I'd like to just ask what it was drove you to the mental hospital, that's all. Was it this Historian you mentioned?

DINKO: What's this?

BETSY: What's what?

DINKO: It's another fork?

(BETSY and DINKO *regard the door frame of the men's entrance. An old newspaper clipping has been tacked to it with a fork.*)

DINKO: *(Looking at photograph in clipping)* It's him.

BETSY: Who?

DINKO: My new roommate. He's staring.

BETSY: That's your roommate?

DINKO: Yeh, they gave me a new roommate last night.

BETSY: Mister Nkumbi?

DINKO: *(Reading)* "Labor Opposition's Barbara Castle protested the Colonial Government's suppression

of Kenya's Mau Mau uprising. She claims evidence
that tens of thousands of Kikuya are in internment
camps and routinely starved and tortured. She cites
the case of a Kikuya leader, a man of great eloquence
among his own people, whose tongue was cut out on
the grounds of a church mission. Alan Lennox-Boyd,
Secretary of State for the Colonies, vigorously denies
these allegations. Meanwhile, Reverend Kenneth
Fullbright of the Territory Inland Mission arrived from
Nairobi this week, accompanied by his American wife.
Reverend Fullbright denies his Mission had a part
in what he claims was an internal affair among the
Kikuya themselves regarding a witch doctor whose
power needed to be curtailed… "
(He pauses. He regards the newspaper photograph.)

BETSY: *(Reading)* "… Reverend Fullbright's role may
indeed be peripheral to these events. The details of
this incidence are unclear and probably can never
be determined. But it is the latest in a long line of
assertions to trouble and embarrass the administration
of Sir Evelyn Baring, Governor of Kenya."

(Pause)

DINKO: Wow. Some story, huh?
Do you think this could really be him now? The
photograph? He could be maybe this witch doctor?

BETSY: Mister Nkumbi?

DINKO: Yeh. My new roommate.

BETSY: I don't know.

DINKO: Yeh? Well, it's been nice to talk. I'm gonna have
to look you up again soon, I promise. *(He slips past*
BETSY. *He exits down the men's hall.)*

*(*BETSY *looks down the hall after him.)*

BETSY: *(Softly)* Mister Dinko?

(No response)

*(*BETSY *regards the newspaper clipping. She removes the fork and clipping. She puts them aside.)*

*(*COOKIE BRAULT *enters from the women's hallway. She holds a bugle and folded flag.)*

COOKIE: What the hell was in your hot chocolate, Fullbright?

BETSY: *(Turning)* Pardon?

COOKIE: Your hot chocolate last night.

BETSY: You tasted my chocolate too?

COOKIE: Damn straight. I always taste your chocolate after I finish mine.

BETSY: So you do, Cookie Brault.

COOKIE: So what'd you haul off and poison it for, Fullbright?

BETSY: I didn't poison. I tasted it too.

COOKIE: That was some powerful medicine, Fullbright, in your hot chocolate.

BETSY: I'm sorry.

COOKIE: You had no business letting anyone else sip it.

*(*COOKIE *steps past* BETSY. *She pulls aside the curtains upstage.* JULIUS *is out on the patio watching television.)*

COOKIE: What the hell's that man doing out there?

BETSY: I'm afraid I don't know, at all, what he's doing.

A VOICE: *(Offstage)* Yoo hoo!

COOKIE: There it is again. That damn yoo hoo.

A VOICE: *(Offstage)* Yoo hoo!

COOKIE: Damn comedian. Mental parrot. What do you suppose, Fullbright, that yoo hoo wants?

BETSY: I'm afraid I don't know.

COOKIE: One phrase is not much to go on, right? Easy to over interpret, eh?

BETSY: Yes, it is.

COOKIE: A whole sentence would be helpful.

A VOICE: *(Offstage)* Yoo hoo! Yoo hoo! Yoo hoo!

(COOKIE opens the sliding glass door.)

COOKIE: You know, Fullbright. I'm beginning to think that yoo hoo can hear what we're saying.
(She exits out onto the patio.)

(Enter DENISE from the downstage entrance.)

DENISE: Betsy Fullbright. Betsy Fullbright. I can find no staff upstairs, no trace anywhere. I can't even find your little in-law that went with me. She's vanished somewhere in the thin air.

(The sound of reveille)

DENISE: But there are wonderful folks upstairs. You would not believe. Upstairs in our home. They said they were coming down. They're on their way down. Right here to meet with you.

(The sound of reveille transforms into choral music.)

(Three figures appear, one at each of the entrances.)

DENISE: There's Elijah, Betsy Fullbright. Look at the prophet Elijah. He's standing there at the entrance to our men's hallway. Not too far, you see, from the picture of Mount Horeb on our wall. Go on, Betsy Fullbright. Wave to Elijah. Wave to him. Wave to the man who went up to heaven in a chariot of fire. To the man who never had to die.
And there's Isaiah of Babylon. At the entrance to our ladies' hall. Did you know, Betsy Fullbright, did you ever realize, that this Isaiah of Babylon was a woman all along? Who could have believed? Who would have

told? That this voice in the wilderness. This huge song. These beautiful feet upon the mountains was a woman all along.

And here's Mary Magdalene, Betsy Fullbright. At this entrance here, can you imagine? The same woman who had seven devils cast out of her. The woman who saw two angels in the sepulcher. Mary Magdalene. Who spoke with them. Who saw a resurrection. And who has now come, she says. Such a long way. To say hello to you.

(MARY MAGDALENE *steps forward. She takes* BETSY's *hand.)*

MARY MAGDALENE: Hello, Betsy Fullbright.

BETSY: Hello?

MARY MAGDALENE: Yes, hello. Dear Betsy Fullbright. *(She kisses* BETSY *on the forehead. She lets go of* BETSY's *hand.)*

(DEUTERO-ISAIAH, ELIJAH, *and* MARY MAGDALENE *head toward the patio door.)*

(DENISE *exits downstage.)*

(DEUTERO-ISAIAH *and* MARY MAGDALENE *stand outside on the patio.* ELIJAH *wheels the television back into the day room.* JULIUS *follows.)*

(Choral music returns again to the sound of reveille.)

(DENISE *enters again downstage.)*

(DEUTERO-ISAIAH, ELIJAH, *and* MARY MAGDALENE *disappear from the patio upstage.)*

DENISE: I can find no staff, Betsy Fullbright.

BETSY: Pardon?

DENISE: Furthermore, I can't even find the in-law you sent with me.

BETSY: Denise?

DENISE: *(Seeing the television)* Oh, my goodness.

BETSY: What?

DENISE: Did you see that? Can you see what I see?

BETSY: Do I see?

DENISE: On the television, yes. It's Mister Nkumbi.

BETSY: Mister Nkumbi?

DENISE: It's Mister Nkumbi walking toward us.

BETSY: Mister Nkumbi doesn't know how to walk.

DENISE: He does on the television.

BETSY: Oh, yes?

DENISE: Yes, and he's speaking. Can you hear what he's speaking?

BETSY: He speaks?

THE TELEVISION: Yoo hoo! Yoo hoo, Mrs Fullbright! YOO HOO! I'm coming, Mrs Fullbright, to get you!

(BETSY and DENISE stare at the television.)

(The sound of reveille continues.)

(The sound of many voices calling out "Yoo hoo!")

(Sound of drums, dancing and chanting)

(JULIUS smiles.)

END OF ACT ONE

ACT TWO

(The same morning)

*(*JULIUS *sits in his wheelchair. He holds a cup, or large mug, in his lap. The cassette player is gone.)*

*(*BETSY *is asleep in a chair at her table. She wakes up.)*

(A retirement home ATTENDANT, *dressed in white, enters from the women's hall.* BETSY *looks up. The* ATTENDANT *crosses the day room and then exits downstage.)*

(Pause)

JULIUS: Welcome back, Mrs Fullbright.

(Pause)

BETSY: Excuse me?

JULIUS: Are you feeling better?

BETSY: Better?

JULIUS: You're feeling better, I can tell.

(Pause)

BETSY: Was I feeling bad?

JULIUS: Bad, yes. You had a temperature.

BETSY: I did?

JULIUS: You were in a fever.

BETSY: Really, a fever?

JULIUS: Oh, yes. You were unconscious for quite some time, I'm afraid.

BETSY: Oh.

JULIUS: Welcome back.

(Pause)

JULIUS: I must confess. I was concerned.

BETSY: Yes?

JULIUS: You spoke frequently.

BETSY: In my fever?

JULIUS: Oh, yes. You said it was hot.

BETSY: What was hot?

JULIUS: The day was hot. As you can see, it is not hot.

BETSY: No, it isn't.

JULIUS: It is quite cool. Cool even for September.

BETSY: Yes.

JULIUS: Certainly cool to be on a picnic.

(Pause)

(BETSY stands. She goes to the sliding glass door upstage. She looks out.)

JULIUS: They have gone.

BETSY: Who?

JULIUS: The yoo hoos.

BETSY: Oh?

JULIUS: For now, yes. They have gone.

BETSY: Yoo hoos, you say?

JULIUS: You were hearing yoo hoos.

BETSY: Was I?

JULIUS: In your fever.

BETSY: You seem to know a lot about my fever.

JULIUS: As I said, you frequently spoke. You complained of hearing yoo hoos.

BETSY: Ah.

JULIUS: From the lawn.

BETSY: Yes, the lawn. I suppose I must have. *(She goes back to her table. She picks up her book. She reads.)*

JULIUS: How is your book?

BETSY: Hm?

JULIUS: The Daniel Bunting book.

BETSY: It's fine.

JULIUS: Do you like it?

BETSY: Well, yes.

JULIUS: I didn't like it.

BETSY: You read my book?

JULIUS: Yes. While you were in your fever.

BETSY: I see.

JULIUS: My people would have killed Daniel Bunting.

BETSY: Your people?

JULIUS: We would not have made him live amongst us.

BETSY: What people?

JULIUS: If I had a people.

BETSY: Ah.

JULIUS: A people who lived in the jungle as in your book.

BETSY: Well, you don't have a people, do you?

JULIUS: We would have killed Daniel Bunting.

BETSY: Good for you. These people didn't. *(She reads. Pause)* I didn't know you could speak.

JULIUS: I speak.

BETSY: Yes, evidently.

JULIUS: I speak, in fact, very clearly.

BETSY: Yes, rather formally, I would say.

JULIUS: I like to be formal.

BETSY: Well, good.

JULIUS: I like to enunciate. Make my thoughts clear.

BETSY: Well, you do very well. With how you speak.

JULIUS: Thank you.

BETSY Somebody's put some time, obviously, yes, into your education.

JULIUS: You think so?

BETSY: Yes. You should be proud.

JULIUS: Yes, I have made much effort. To learn your language.
To become fluent.

BETSY: Well, it shows. *(She reads.)*

*(*JULIUS *watches.)*

JULIUS: I must say I have come to like your language. Yes. I am fond of it.
I didn't expect so. I thought to learn your language would be difficult. An unpleasant, distasteful task.
But I have come to think of your language as a very thick language. It has a thick underbrush to it. There are so many places to hide in your language. A whole forest of thoughts and words, and no clear, lasting path anywhere. It is wonderful how one can hide and sneak and lurk in your language. There are all these places. To be never seen. These nooks and crannies. From which to speak one thing, or to make some noise over here, faraway from where you actually are. This

was a revelation to me. If I were a leopard, and your
language were a jungle, then your language would be
my favorite jungle, my favorite spot on earth, my best
hunting ground, my deepest nighttime, to look for
food, or stalk, as they say, for prey.
Oh, yes.
And if I were indeed this leopard, and your language
were indeed my jungle, my happy hunting ground,
my deepest night-time, then I know for sure a day
will sometime dawn, when I will walk to the edge of
this jungle. I will come to where all the jungle ends.
Come out of the deepest nighttime. And before me I
will see an open plain. Immense with many creatures,
with elephants, lion and antelope. Zebras and giraffe.
A multitude of such creatures, as in the ages ago. But
in all this immensity of creatures I will notice, I know,
just one tiny creature. A young goat. A kid. Who has
lost the company she keeps. A straggler. Who has
wandered, I see, faraway from a farm, an enclosure for
goats and sheep, where she was meant to stay. And
she has come now. Much too close to the edge of this
forest. Where I have come now to lurk.
*(Pause. He takes a sip from the cup in his lap. He makes a
quiet slurp.)*

BETSY: *(Looking up)* Mister Nkumbi?

JULIUS: Yes, Mrs Fullbright?

BETSY: I'm trying to read. Do you mind?

JULIUS: Of course, not. I'm happy if you read.

BETSY: Thank you.

JULIUS: It's good, of course, to hide oneself from time to
time. In a book.

(BETSY reads.)

*(JULIUS sips from his cup. He makes a quiet slurp. He
watches BETSY.)*

BETSY: *(Looking up)* You're staring, Mister Nkumbi.

JULIUS: Oh?

BETSY: You shouldn't stare. You always stare.

JULIUS: When have I stared?

BETSY: In my fever, you stared.

JULIUS: *(Pleased)* You remember?

BETSY: Of course, I remember.

JULIUS: A leopard stares.

BETSY: Oh?

JULIUS: Yes, before he strikes. It is a form of mesmerism.

BETSY: What is this fancy of yours, Mister Nkumbi?

JULIUS: What fancy?

BETSY: You fancy yourself, do you? As a leopard?

JULIUS: Well, perhaps I do. I could confess.

BETSY: You should have played more as a child.

JULIUS: But who knows, then, one's true fancy?

BETSY: Played leopard, yes, in the woods. Got it out of your system.

JULIUS: I'm not playing, Mrs Fullbright. You are in danger.

BETSY: Danger, am I?

JULIUS: Your people are at the picnic.

BETSY: I know they're at the picnic.

JULIUS: You are like a straggler to me. You are left behind.

BETSY: Behind where?

JULIUS: You would feel better were you at the picnic. In your enclosure, so to speak.

BETSY: I feel fine.

JULIUS: I'm glad you feel so fine.

BETSY: Why aren't you at the picnic? Don't you like picnics?

JULIUS: I like them somewhat.

BETSY: You wanted to stay here and talk leopard?

JULIUS: I told them I wanted to rest.

BETSY: Who, the staff?

JULIUS: I arrived, yes, last night. Just before they served the hot chocolate.

BETSY: Oh?

JULIUS: From Nairobi.

BETSY: You came from Nairobi?

JULIUS: Yes, I did.

BETSY: All the way from there?

JULIUS: You know Nairobi?

BETSY: What brought you here from Nairobi?

JULIUS: I was asked to come.

BETSY: To this country?

JULIUS: Yes. To this facility.

BETSY: This particular facility?

JULIUS: Oh, yes. I was asked by my ancestors.

BETSY: Your what?

JULIUS: My ancestors asked me.

BETSY: Oh? And how did they manage that?

JULIUS: Well, they came to me, of course. In a vision.

BETSY: Ah. A vision.

JULIUS: The voice of my ancestors told me to come here. They made the arrangements.

BETSY: Your ancestors did?

JULIUS: They arranged it, yes.

BETSY: The airplane flight, I assume? The visas, passport, ground transportation, all that?

JULIUS: Oh, yes.

BETSY: I didn't know all that could get arranged. In a vision.

JULIUS: It can, yes.

BETSY: But this particular retirement facility doesn't accept, I believe, transfers from Nairobi. Or recommendations from ancestors, for that matter.

JULIUS: The voice of my ancestors can arrange these things.

BETSY: Oh? Must be convenient, then.

JULIUS: You think so?

BETSY: Oh, yes, to have such ancestors. To hear such a voice. To have such a sweet, charming belief in such things.

JULIUS: Well, I'm glad, then. You feel so charmed, Mrs. Fullbright.

(BETSY *returns to reading.*)

(*Pause*)

JULIUS: Would you like some hot chocolate?

(*No response.*)

JULIUS: I'm having hot chocolate. Would you care to join me?

BETSY: (*Reading*) No, thank you. I'm trying to finish my book, actually.

(JULIUS *sips from his cup. He makes a quiet slurp. He*
watches BETSY.)

(BETSY *stirs. She concentrates on reading.*)

JULIUS: I came once to the ocean.
I knew if I went to this ocean. I could wait on the shore.
For a boat to come with cargo.
A cargo boat from my ancestors.
And so I waited on this shore. With hardly food to eat.
Each day I saw many ships, but no boat, I could tell,
from my ancestors. But I knew I must not move, no,
from this spot on the shore.
I must wait. And then one night I heard it. On the
ocean, I saw, in the moonlight, I knew, a boat from my
ancestors. And I saw the Spirit of one ancestor come
ashore. The Spirit said to me, We have no ammunition.
No weapon, no invulnerability, can we find to give to
you. And I said, Why? How have I waited so long for
you to come ashore? Where is the cargo to take back to
my people? How can I gather my lost people again? If I
have no cargo?
And I fell at the feet of the Spirit. I thought I will never
stand again. I cannot. I will lie here on the shore until I
become bones. I am dust.
But the Spirit took my hand and lifted me. And when
I was on my feet, I saw I was no longer ashore. I was
myself on the cargo boat. I saw the shore faraway and
for a moment I saw my people. All my people gathered
together on this boat. They welcomed me aboard. And
then my people were gone. I saw they vanished. And
we began to sail away. And I said, No. I cannot sail
away like this to join the ancestors. Without my people.
I must return. I will search both this world and the lost
worlds until I gather my people.
And then the boat was gone. I was alone again on the
shore to the ocean. But I saw there was a small leopard

cub. Asleep at my feet. And I knew this was my cargo.
Given to me by my ancestors. This leopard cub is my
cargo. I must open it to see. And so I broke open the
neck of the leopard cub. And when I broke its neck,
I saw its Spirit assemble in the air beside me. I saw it
would now accompany me, wherever I must go. I saw
it could instruct me. It will teach me to be silent. Teach
me to find my prey. It will teach me the moment to
pounce.
And now I hear a voice. Which does not leave me. It is
with me everywhere. The voice of my ancestors. Who
watch faraway from the shore. Who see what I cannot
see. Who told me to set out on a journey. We had a
journey to make, this leopard and I.
I have come now to the end of my journey.

(Pause)

(A dark animal, or LEOPARD, *moves past the patio door
outside. It disappears.)*

(The resonant sound of a leopard's snarl.)

*(*BETSY *looks up from her reading. She stares at the patio
door. She looks at* JULIUS, *who has closed his eyes. He might
be sleeping.)*

BETSY: Mister Nkumbi? Did you once have a cassette
player? There in your lap?

A VOICE: *(Offstage)* Yoo hoo!

(Pause)

*(*JULIUS *opens his eyes.)*

JULIUS: You heard the yoo hoo?

BETSY: Yes?

JULIUS: My ancestors.

BETSY: Out there on the lawn?

JULIUS: They are calling to us.

BETSY: Calling?

JULIUS: You must listen, I think.

BETSY: Ancestors don't go yoo hoo.

JULIUS: They wish you to listen.

BETSY: Whatever for?

JULIUS: You have no choice.

A VOICE: *(Offstage)* Yoo hoo!

(JULIUS closes his eyes. He smiles.)

(BETSY stares at him.)

(DENISE enters from the women's hall.)

BETSY: Denise Jones, did you hear that?

DENISE: Morning, Betsy Fullbright.

BETSY: Denise, did you?

DENISE: Did I what?

BETSY: Hear a yoo hoo?

DENISE: A yoo hoo?

BETSY: Yes.

DENISE: What do you mean, hear a yoo hoo?

BETSY: You didn't hear someone just now? Call out yoo hoo?

DENISE: I didn't hear no yoo hoo.

A VOICE: *(Offstage)* Yoo hoo!

(DENISE goes to the television. She turns it on.)

BETSY: Well, they just did it again.

DENISE: Did what?

BETSY: Someone just now shouted yoo hoo.

DENISE: They did?

BETSY: You didn't hear?

DENISE: Betsy Fullbright, I didn't hear nothing.

BETSY: I see. Well, Mister Nkumbi heard a yoo hoo.

DENISE: Did he?

BETSY: Mister Nkumbi, didn't you hear a yoo hoo?

DENISE: Mister. Nkumbi doesn't speak.

BETSY: Excuse me?

DENISE: They told me in the Nurses' Office last night.

BETSY: But he spoke.

DENISE: When?

BETSY: To me. He spoke.

DENISE: He has no voice with which to speak. They told me.

BETSY: What do you mean, he has no voice?

DENISE: He lost it in a hospital.

BETSY: What hospital?

DENISE: Some place overseas. His vocal chords is cut.

BETSY: But this man spoke to me. He told me I had a fever this morning. He talked to me about his ancestors. He was quite explicit that he was from Nairobi and that he had ancestors. Who purchased his plane ticket here. From Nairobi.

(Pause)

DENISE: Uh huh. You must have just thought he spoke. *(She takes a seat in front of the television.)*

(Pause)

BETSY: What are you watching?

DENISE: The news.

BETSY: But there's no sound.

DENISE: Hm?

BETSY: The television's obviously broken.

DENISE: It has sound.

BETSY: The television has?

DENISE: Uh huh.

BETSY: Funny. I don't hear it.

DENISE: You don't hear this sound?

BETSY: No, I don't.

DENISE: You don't hear all this news?

BETSY: That doesn't look like news.

DENISE: No?

BETSY: It's a picnic. I see a picnic.

DENISE: Picnic?

BETSY: Yes.

DENISE: What kind of picnic?

BETSY: Our picnic. The one we're supposed to be at.

DENISE: On the television?

BETSY: You don't see it? Our picnic?

DENISE: No. I see the news.

BETSY: Oh.

DENISE: Uh huh. Just news.

BETSY: Well, I'm certainly not hearing anything.

DENISE: Then how come you hear me, Betsy Fullbright?
But not the news?

BETSY: I wouldn't know.

DENISE: You seem spooked.

BETSY: Pardon?

DENISE: You seem very spooked this morning.

BETSY: Spooked? Well, perhaps I am.

DENISE: Just a spell, I'm sure. It'll pass. *(Pause. She watches the television.)*

BETSY: Denise? Did you feel ill this morning?

DENISE: Ill? Yeah, I was ill. I didn't want no picnic anyway.

BETSY: Was it because, you think, of my hot chocolate?

DENISE: Your what?

BETSY: Did you taste my hot chocolate last night?

DENISE: I tasted it, yeah.

BETSY: Do you think it made you sick?

DENISE: What, hot chocolate?

BETSY: It didn't taste bad?

DENISE: It tasted fine. *(She sees* JULIUS. *She stands.)* Oh, I'm sorry, Mister Nkumbi. You should be over here with me. So we can watch television together. *(To* BETSY*)* The nurses said last night to let Mister Nkumbi watch television with me. We're television buddies. *(She goes to* JULIUS. *She takes a hold of his wheelchair. Looking through patio door)* Well, look at that. Look at the goat out there.

BETSY: A goat?

DENISE: Yeah, somebody left a goat on our lawn. A little baby goat. A kid. All sweet and grazing. At the end of our lawn.

BETSY: Why would there be a goat?

DENISE: I don't know. I can see no tether.

BETSY: Oh?

DENISE: Could be just out wandering. It has no business being alone, that baby goat. There could be dogs around here. Or nasty children. It could wander too onto a highway nearby. I should tell the staff.

Somebody should go out and rescue that goat. One of the staff should chase it down. *(To* JULIUS*)* Excuse me, Mister Nkumbi. I'll be back to watch television with you. After I get some staff.

(She exits downstage.)

*(*BETSY *stands. She goes to the patio door. She looks out. She lingers at the patio door. She regards* JULIUS*, whose eyes are closed. She goes to the bookcase and sees a cassette player on one of the shelves. She puts it on a table. She presses the PLAY button.)*

(The sound of the National Anthem.)

*(*BETSY *presses the STOP button. She puts the cassette player back. She regards the television.)*

*(*JULIUS *opens his eyes.)*

JULIUS: How's the news?

BETSY: *(Turning)* What?

JULIUS: I said, The news.

BETSY: I see a picnic.

JULIUS: Hm.

BETSY: Do you see a picnic?

JULIUS: Denise Jones is correct, by the way.

BETSY: About the news?

JULIUS: I do not speak. I have no vocal chords.

BETSY: Oh?

JULIUS: I have no physical means left with which to speak.

BETSY: And yet you speak? Your lips move?

JULIUS: Yes. You certainly hear me.

BETSY: But you're not speaking?

JULIUS: Well, you and I know, of course, that I speak. I speak very clearly. But no one else knows. They will never know.

BETSY: No?

JULIUS: Yes. I am your secret friend. We are imaginary friends together. This is our secret, our knowledge of what is true, which no one else will believe. They will think instead you have taken to talking to yourself. Can you imagine? Thinking so? Because they are not deep. Like you and I. Who are deep. So deep, so smart looking, we can't even hear the television sound, what you were once accustomed to. Those reassuring noises escape you now. For example, the Muzak. We do not hear muzak, do we?

BETSY: Muzak? No?

JULIUS: If you ask Denise Jones, she will tell you there is muzak.

BETSY: Really?

JULIUS: Oh, yes. Really. *(He raises one hand. He waves his pinky finger.)*

(The sound of Muzak)

JULIUS: Do you like the tune, Downtown?

BETSY: Do I like it?

JULIUS: They are playing Downtown.

BETSY: Yes, of course. Downtown.

(JULIUS waves his pinky again.)

(The sound of Muzak stops.)

JULIUS: Of course, we are not hearing Downtown. Nor do we see the news. We see a picnic. We see me, of course, talking with you.

(Pause. BETSY *sits down at her table.)*

BETSY: Mister Nkumbi?

JULIUS: Yes, Mrs Fullbright?

BETSY: I'm not amused. At all by this.

JULIUS: Oh?

BETSY: You appear to be amused.

JULIUS: Yes. I'm sorry.

BETSY: Nor am I afraid of you. Whoever you are.

JULIUS: Ah. But you know who I am.

BETSY: No, I don't think I do.

JULIUS: Well, then. I intend for you to remember. You
should be remembering, I think, rather soon.
(Pause)
Would you like some hot chocolate? I'm having hot
chocolate.

BETSY: No, thank you.

JULIUS: I'm sorry to have just one cup, Mrs Fullbright.
But perhaps you would share this cup with me. Over
our table here.

BETSY: *(Standing)* Well, that's sweet of you, Mister
Nkumbi. But what I'd like, actually, is to be left alone.
With my own thoughts. I've had enough, for now, I
think, of conversing with you. And so I hope you will
excuse me, please. If I insist for now on being alone.
(She goes to JULIUS. *She takes a hold of his wheelchair.
She wheels him to the patio door. She opens it. She pushes*
JULIUS *out onto the patio. She closes the door. She closes the
curtains. She regards the television. She goes to it and turns
it off. The television won't turn off. She pulls the plug. The
picnic remains on the screen. She turns the television around
to face the wall. She regards the silent Muzak speaker on the
wall.)*

(Enter DINKO *from the men's hall. He tiptoes along the wall of the day room towards the women's hall.)*

BETSY: Ah. Mister Dinko.

DINKO: *(Turning)* Who's that?

BETSY: On your way again, I see, to the ladies' hall?

DINKO: Who, me?

BETSY: *(Cheerful)* Looking again, are you, for the troublemaker?

DINKO: *(Suspicious)* What troublemaker?

BETSY: The yoo hooer.

DINKO: The yoo hooer? I know nothing about a yoo hooer.

BETSY: Well, but you did say there was trouble.

DINKO: We have never spoken before, I'm sure.

BETSY: Yes, you told me about Moses. The trouble with Moses.

DINKO: What trouble?

BETSY: Oh, come on, Mister Dinko. You told me about the Great Redactor.

DINKO: I did?

BETSY: Something about Deuteronomy. And some gang.

DINKO: Wow.

BETSY: Pardon?

DINKO: That's confidential. I took you so soon into my confidence? You must be quite a lady. Probably you can cast quite a spell.

BETSY: Yes, you said that.

DINKO: What else did I confide in you?

BETSY: You said you'd been to Havana.

DINKO: Yeh? I was something standing in the streets of Havana. We could have got married, by the way.

BETSY: I don't think so, no.

DINKO: No, really, I know how to handle a lady with a spell.

BETSY: I see.

DINKO: We should talk more often, I think, with the curtains closed like so. I was written up, you know, in Havana with ladies like you.

BETSY: Ah, please. Mister Dinko.

DINKO: This is a hell of a spell.

BETSY: What is?

DINKO: What I'm feeling now for you.

BETSY: Easy now.

DINKO: What's the matter? You don't feel this spell too?

BETSY: No, actually, I don't.

DINKO: You need to talk about Moses first?

BETSY: Pardon?

DINKO: You want me to tell you about the Deuteronomistic Historian?

BETSY: Well, actually.

DINKO: That could cast the spell for you too? That could make you go crazy for me?

BETSY: Mister Dinko.

DINKO: What's that?

BETSY: What's what?

DINKO: I think you have a fork in there. In your blouse.

BETSY: I have a fork?

DINKO: Somebody left a fork there.

BETSY: They did not.

DINKO: Here, I'll show you.

BETSY: Get your hands off me.

DINKO: I'm reaching, that's all, for the fork.

BETSY: You stay where you are.

DINKO: Okay. I'm gonna circle around over here.

BETSY: Thank you.

DINKO: Did you find it yet?

BETSY: What?

DINKO: The fork in your blouse.

BETSY: *(Holding fork)* Yes, I did.

DINKO: What's it doing there?

BETSY: How should I know?

DINKO: Okay. Well, we got that one out of the way. You ready for a smooch?

BETSY: Get back. Stay away.

DINKO: You want me to hold the fork first? After you?

BETSY: What?

DINKO: You need to hold a fork before we nooky?

BETSY: No, never! Out, you rowdy!

DINKO: *(Sweetly)* I can tell you're probably out of touch with your longing for me.

BETSY: *(Grabbing cassette player from bookcase)* Mister Dinko!

DINKO: Yeh, I never met a lady before. Who keeps a fork like this between her breast.

BETSY: Stop!

(BETSY *brings the cassette player down on* DINKO's *head.
He falls to the ground unconscious. She regards the smashed
cassette player. She puts it back on the shelf. She regards
him. She takes him by the feet and drags him into the men's
hall. She exits, dragging him.*)

(*Enter* JULIUS *from the reception area downstage. He has a
tray on his lap. It holds a large pot and three large cups. He
wheels upstage. He puts the tray on* BETSY's *table. He wheels
over to the television. He turns it around, facing the room
again. There is still a picnic on the screen. He turns to the
patio. He opens the patio curtains. He wheels himself back to*
BETSY's *table.*)

(*Enter* BETSY *from the men's hall.*)

JULIUS: Ah. Mrs Fullbright.
You've come back in time, I think. For some hot
chocolate.
(*He takes the pot and pours hot chocolate into two of the
cups.*)
Come. I assure you. There is nothing in this hot
chocolate. Just nasty rumors, that's all. I drink it all the
time myself.
Please. Join me at your table.
(*He puts aside the pot. He regards the third cup.*)
I am expecting, of course, a third person. Your
husband.

BETSY: My husband?

JULIUS: Oh, yes. He said he might show up. For hot
chocolate.

BETSY: My husband's been deceased. For some time
now.

JULIUS: Well. He said he would like to be here anyway.
For hot chocolate. And if he cannot come, if his new
schedule does not permit, then he promised, at least, to

send his regrets. We will be able, you and I, of course, to share his regrets.

(*He sips from the his cup. He makes a quiet slurp. He watches* BETSY.)

What would you like to talk about? While we wait here?

Perhaps for your husband's regrets?

(*No response.*)

(JULIUS *regards the patio door.*)

JULIUS: I think we should talk about the weather. That's always good for a subject.

All this stranger weather, yes?

This morning was cold. And now all of a sudden, it's hot. Hot, I think, like Africa. Or a biblical land. Tell me. Is it spring or winter out there? Summer or fall? Every day now makes its own rules. Its own weather. All the boundaries are gone. The little enclosures.

(BETSY *steps briskly across the room. She comes to her table. She takes a hold of* JULIUS*'s wheelchair.*)

BETSY: I think it's time, Mister Nkumbi, don't you? To send you to your room. You're obviously being a nuisance in here.

(BETSY *attempts to move* JULIUS*'s wheelchair. It doesn't budge. She attempts to move it again. It still doesn't budge. He sits, calmly watching.*)

JULIUS: You may be good at removing forks, at my discretion. But if I decide, you cannot move me.

BETSY: If you decide?

JULIUS: It's impossible, Mrs Fullbright. I assure you.

(BETSY *glares at* JULIUS. *She steps back briskly across the room. She regards the bookcase. She removes a book from a shelf. She sits down at a table. She reads.*)

(JULIUS *regards the television. The picnic is gone from the screen. Instead, there are pictures of various reptiles and creatures.*)

JULIUS: Ah. They found a snake with two heads in a swamp, did you know? It is on the local news. And what could that mean? What is going on, they say, with these mutations. These frogs with extra legs. Those turtles now with four tails.

Perhaps it is no longer so far to go for a creature to have seven heads and ten horns. Even the body, let's say, of a leopard, but with the footsies of a bear, and the mouth of a lion. Like what it says in the book of Revelation. Yes. I think that is what has come to inhabit our land. Beasts could be like that. Lurking around here, you know. Just beyond our view.

(*He regards* BETSY *across the room.*)

JULIUS: (*Softly*) Yoo hoo, Mrs Fullbright.
I know what you are reading. What book you are trying to hide yourself in now.

BETSY: (*Reading*) Hm?

JULIUS: Your Bible.

BETSY: (*Looking up*) My Bible?

JULIUS: Yes. You found a Bible over there. On the shelf.

BETSY: Yes. I most certainly did.
(*She reads.*)

JULIUS: Have you heard, Mrs Fullbright, of spiritual wickedness?

BETSY: Spiritual wickedness?

JULIUS: Yes. In high places?

BETSY: Well, yes. I have.

JULIUS: Have you had experience with this? With spiritual wickedness in high places?

BETSY: No. Not that I recall.

JULIUS: You don't recall?

BETSY: No, sorry.
(She reads.)

JULIUS: You are very brave, Mrs Fullbright. I think I would be brave too if I were you.

(BETSY stirs. She concentrates on reading.)

JULIUS: You must admit I am deep. Beyond the bland friendly surface of these words I say, it is deep, O, so deep.
Perhaps I am your real intended. What should have been, who could know? I who am deep. And who could make you deep too. Who could light up all your dark corners, inner recesses. All the nooks and crannies where you have never thought or maybe dared to look.
(He sips from his cup. He makes a quiet slurp.)
We are the mere surface, you and I, sipping chocolate, of what could be deep.
Do you enjoy talking like this? About what is deep?

BETSY: I think you're the only one talking here, really.

JULIUS: Ah, yes.

BETSY: Which hardly makes a conversation.

JULIUS: I know. I'm sorry. I wish to engage you.

BETSY: I suppose you think you're being rather ominous.

JULIUS: Ominous?

BETSY: Well, these things you say.

JULIUS: No, I think I'm being very friendly. Almost frisky.

BETSY: I think you just fancy yourself, that's all. As that leopard of yours. Lurking around over there in your words.

JULIUS: Ah. You flatter me.

BETSY: All this nonsense. About being deep.

JULIUS: You don't think so?

BETSY: Listen, Mister Nkumbi. You know the thing that's got me through before? No matter what.

JULIUS: No?

BETSY: It's my humor. I have humor, I do. I may not always show it. But inside there's humor. There's resolve. In all my nooks and crannies I have humor. I can break out and laugh. Right in the face of anything. I've done it often before.

JULIUS: You care to laugh?

BETSY: Yes. I'll laugh.

JULIUS: And what will that do? If you laugh?

BETSY: It will break this spell. Whatever's going on with the television, or the muzak, this mesmerism. This need to hear you talking to me.

JULIUS: Ah. You would like more gaiety and laughter, then? Over our chocolate.

BETSY: Not at all, no.

JULIUS: No, please. Let me see, Mrs Fullbright, I think. What I can do for you. For our gaiety and laughter. *(He raises one hand. He waves his pinky finger.)*

(The sound of Muzak. Downtown)

(UDAYA DAWN enters downstage, tiptoeing and dancing.)

(Enter DINKO from the men's hallway and enter COOKIE and DENISE from the women's hallway. They tiptoe and dance across the stage.)

(BETSY gets up abruptly. She crosses the dayroom and exits down the women's hall.)

(*Exit* COOKIE, DENISE, DINKO, *and* UDAYA DAWN *tiptoeing and dancing.*)

(BETSY *reappears at the women's entrance.*)

(JULIUS *waves his pinky.*)

(*The Muzak stops.*)

(*Pause*)

JULIUS: You did not like that, Mrs Fullbright? You don't like our gaiety? All our laughter?

BETSY: No, Mister Nkumbi. No, I do not.

JULIUS: Oh. I am sorry, then.

BETSY: What has happened to my room?

JULIUS: Your room?

BETSY: Yes. My room down the hall.

JULIUS: You misplaced your room?

BETSY: No, it's gone. There's no door anywhere to my room.

JULIUS: Oh?

BETSY: No windows. The room's gone.

JULIUS: Hm. Perhaps, Mrs Fullbright, you won't be needing that room anymore.

BETSY: Won't be needing?

JULIUS: If it has disappeared like so.

BETSY: No, actually, I'd like to be left alone. Very much so. All alone.

JULIUS: In your room?

BETSY: Yes.

JULIUS: Ah. I think, more deeply, actually, you want to talk about Kenneth.

BETSY: Who?

JULIUS: Your dear husband. You hope to hear something from him. Even a little word. Perhaps you think he should come here, like a séance, and rescue you.

BETSY: Rescue?

JULIUS: Oh, yes. Kenneth could always do that. Step between you and danger. Any doubts. Or second thoughts. Nagging misgivings. Kenneth was always so good to step in. To put in perspective. If things began to look maybe a little too deep.

(Pause)

BETSY: You have no idea what you're talking about. You should learn to keep quiet. When you have nothing to say.
(She goes back to the table by the bookcase. She picks up the book.)
(With resolve) I must learn too. To resist this absurd, illogical temptation.
(She sits down. She reads.)

JULIUS: What temptation, Mrs Fullbright?

(No response)

JULIUS: This murky need, as you say, to hear me talking to you?
To give in, let's say, to a certain disorientation?
Or need to question?

(No response)

JULIUS: I'm afraid this alternative you seek might not be so comforting either.
If I should keep quiet. As you say.
I could be your only rescue, you know. From what is now, O, much too deep.

(COOKIE enters from the women's hallway. She regards BETSY.)

(BETSY *looks up warily.*)

(JULIUS *grins. He nods.*)

COOKIE: You looked spooked, Fullbright.

BETSY: Pardon?

COOKIE: I said, Spooked.

BETSY   No. I'm not spooked, no.

COOKIE: Yeah, ashen. Your face is ashen.

BETSY: I'm not ashen, no, at all.

COOKIE: Lost some of that flouncy color to your cheeks, have you, Fullbright?

BETSY: I'm sorry?

COOKIE: Yeah? Who's this new gink?

BETSY: New gink?

COOKIE: *(Indicating* JULIUS*)* Him?

BETSY: Oh. I'm afraid I don't know at all who that man is.

(JULIUS *grins. He nods toward the large pot on the table next to him.*)

COOKIE: *(To* JULIUS*)* Thank you, yeah. I think I will.
(She pours herself a cup of hot chocolate. She drinks. She makes a quiet slurp.)
Have you seen the staff, Fullbright?

BETSY: The staff? No.

COOKIE: I'm looking for staff.

BETSY: I believe Denise Jones might be looking for them too.

COOKIE: *(Slurping)* Uh huh.

BETSY: I saw one earlier.

COOKIE: One what?

BETSY: One staff.

COOKIE: Uh huh.
(She puts the cup back down on the table. She exits downstage, humming 'Downtown.')

(Pause)

(JULIUS smiles.)

(The sound of choral music.)

(DEUTERO-ISAIAH, ELIJAH and MARY MAGDALENE appear on the patio outside. They regard BETSY in the dayroom. BETSY stirs, uncomfortable. ELIJAH opens the patio door. He walks over to the framed picture of the mountain top. He adjusts it, tilting it to one side. He goes to the table near JULIUS. He takes a sip of hot chocolate from the cup. He exits back out onto the patio.)

(COOKIE enters downstage.)

COOKIE: Damn, Fullbright. How the hell did it get so bright in here?

BETSY: *(Standing)* Bright?

COOKIE: *(Going to patio door)* Damn, that's bright out there. Look at that lawn. Must be about to blister. Or boil. What's making the sky so blasted luminous today?
(She closes the patio door curtains.)
Must be our eyes, huh, Fullbright? Can't be an extra sun or two, huh, just showed up in the sky today? Can't be seven days of sun, no, all in one day? Hell, no, must be this damn perception thing again.
(She exits down the women's hall.)

(Pause)

(BETSY sits down. She stares at the crooked picture on the wall. She stares at her book. She reads.)

JULIUS: How is your book?

(No response)

JULIUS: Is your book fine?

(No response)

JULIUS: I know what you have been reading. I can see
it, O, so clearly from here. As if I were a little bird
perched on your shoulder. As if I were your own
thoughts. And what my little bird tells me is about
Elijah. Who was like Moses. Once upon a time on
the mountain top. That mountain on the wall, Betsy
Fullbright. Where Elijah first heard a still, small voice.
Underneath all the wind, the earthquake, the fire, was
just a still, small voice.
How is your still, small voice, Betsy Fullbright? Can
you hear it? Does it talk to you? Like a small voice of
conscience?
Or is it gone? Do you hear now no such small voice?
Only a yoo hoo instead?

A VOICE: *(Offstage)* Yoo hoo!

(BETSY turns pages in her book. She reads more.)

JULIUS: Ah. You think you can hide from me. But
my birdie is still there. Watching on your shoulder.
And what my birdie tells is you are reading Isaiah.
The voice in the wilderness. Her beautiful feet on the
mountains.

A VOICE: *(Offstage)* Yoo hoo!

(BETSY turns more pages.)

JULIUS: Ah. And now you see Mary Magdalene. She is
weeping outside the sepulcher. And now she speaks to
a gardener. She doesn't know this gardener is Jesus. It's
Jesus now who speaks to her.

A VOICE: *(Offstage)* Yoo hoo!

JULIUS: It's terrible, I know, what you cannot read. If you hear a yoo hoo instead. And where, O, where can all this yoo hoo come from, Betsy Fullbright?

(BETSY *stares at* JULIUS.)

JULIUS: I will ask you again. Have you heard, Betsy Fullbright, of spiritual wickedness? In high places?

BETSY: Spiritual wickedness?

JULIUS: Yes. Have you had experience with this? With such wickedness?

BETSY: No. Not that I recall.

JULIUS: You don't recall?

BETSY: No.

JULIUS: Well. It's a very dangerous thing to use that book you hold. I can tell you. For your own purposes.

A VOICE: *(Offstage)* Yoo hoo!

JULIUS: I have studied your book, Betsy Fullbright. It was the way I could track you down. If I studied this book. I could find where you hide.
It is a very confusing book, I admit. They say it's redacted, you have, of course, heard. There is a Deuteronomistic Historian, a Chronicler, all sorts of conflicting prophets and priests. There is Paul, and then there is Deutero-Paul, who is not Paul, but someone later, sprinkled all over everywhere. It's a bloody mess, your book. This book you hold claims to be about one God, but actually there are many Gods arguing in here to be the one God. How could the God who tells about the wolf and the lamb dwelling together, be the same God, who orders the slaughter of nations who were residing there first in a promised land? All the slaughter of the Canaanites? Or how could the God, who tells about the leopard lying down with the billy goat kid, also order the Assyrians and

Babylonians to destroy his own people? What possible expression of intelligence or integrity could any of this be? What possible promise could such a land have?
No, it is conflated. It is more than one witness.
Because one of these Gods is not God. And they are arguing right there in that book. Arguing it out for all the world to see.
Asking us to distinguish, right there in this book, what is not God from what is God.
(Pause)
I have come to like the still, small voice.
I like too the voice in the wilderness. The beautiful feet on the mountains.
I like the lady weeping outside the sepulcher.
I like, too, that there may be a way somewhere. To overcome death.

A VOICE: *(Offstage)* Yoo hoo!

JULIUS: *(Softly)* Betsy Fullbright?

BETSY: Yes?

JULIUS: I think I see them. Your husband's regrets.

BETSY: His regrets?

JULIUS: He must have come by earlier and left them.

BETSY: Where?

JULIUS: There's an envelope up there.

BETSY: What envelope?

JULIUS: Behind the picture.

(BETSY looks up at the picture on the wall. An envelope sticks out from behind the frame.)

(The sound of Muzak.)

(BETSY is startled. She looks up at the speaker on the wall. She looks around the room. She sees the television screen. It's

*gone dead. She goes over to the television. She puts the plug
in. She turns it on. The screen lights up.)*

(The sound of the television.)

(BETSY turns the television off. The sound stops.)

(BETSY opens the curtains. She opens the patio door.)

(BETSY regards JULIUS, whose eyes are closed.)

(The sound of Muzak continues.)

BETSY: Mister Nkumbi?

(No response)

*(BETSY regards the picture on the wall. She takes the
envelope from behind the frame. She opens it. She reads. She
bursts out laughing.)*

(Enter UDAYA DAWN from the reception area downstage.)

UDAYA DAWN: Auntie?

(BETSY continues laughing. She is hysterical.)

(UDAYA DAWN goes to her.)

UDAYA DAWN: Auntie. Auntie. Come, please, Auntie.
What is wrong?
Come, please. We must sit. Sit, Auntie, here.

(UDAYA DAWN sits with BETSY at a table.)

UDAYA DAWN: What is wrong, Auntie?

BETSY: I found this letter.

UDAYA DAWN: Yes, I see.

BETSY: It was behind the picture here.

UDAYA DAWN: Yes?

BETSY: It's from my husband.

UDAYA DAWN: This letter from your husband was
behind the picture here?

BETSY: Yes, it was.

UDAYA DAWN: And this made you cry, or hysterical somewhat?

BETSY: Dawn?

UDAYA DAWN: Yes, Auntie?

BETSY: I don't know your name.

UDAYA DAWN: Pardon, Auntie?

BETSY: What is your other name? Your name?

UDAYA DAWN: Udaya?

BETSY: Yes, Udaya. Please, who are you? I don't know why you visit.

UDAYA DAWN: I'm your grand-niece, Auntie.

BETSY: My grand-niece?

UDAYA DAWN: Yes.

BETSY: I wasn't sure.

UDAYA DAWN: That's okay.

BETSY: How did you find me here, Udaya?

UDAYA DAWN: I go to school nearby. I was told.

BETSY: School?

UDAYA DAWN: Yes, university.

BETSY: Would you read this letter, Udaya, please?

UDAYA DAWN: Oh, no. I'm sure it's private.

BETSY: Please. Read to me. I'd like to hear it. Hear someone read it. It's from my husband. Some years ago.

UDAYA DAWN: Yes, Auntie. Of course.
(She takes the letter from BETSY.)
(Reading) "My dearest darling Elizabeth. I am sorry I must be so faraway again. Like this from you. I regret how you must continue to bear up on your own under these circumstances. While I make yet another

journey into the interior. Quell the unrest they tell
us now is growing there. In this darkest of corners in
the universe. And I promise when I come back it will
be with the same sure knowledge that what we do,
and how we go about it, is God's will. I do thank you,
darling, for your support these last several months. I
don't know how I could have managed without you.
Without your steadfast trust. Your deep refusal to
believe all those lies about me. Those rumors regarding
that man we finally chased out of here. I believe it was
your obvious example of devotion, innocence and
fidelity that ultimately served to clear my name.
"Your loving husband, Kenneth."
(She hands the letter back to BETSY.*)*
It's a nice letter. Very nice, Auntie. It made you cry?

BETSY: He's lying, Udaya.

UDAYA DAWN: Pardon?

BETSY: This letter is a lie.

UDAYA DAWN: Oh.

BETSY: I did not see it before.

UDAYA DAWN: I'm sorry, Auntie. If it is a lie.

BETSY: I did not see it. What spirit moved me not to
see? How could it take this long, utterly horribly long,
to see what's been staring all along at me? Right in the
eyes.

UDAYA DAWN: Auntie?

BETSY: Mister Nkumbi?

UDAYA DAWN: Auntie, please.

BETSY: Mister Nkumbi, Mister Nkumbi.
(She stands. She goes to JULIUS *at the other table.)*
Mister Nkumbi?
(She sits down at his feet.)

Mister Nkumbi, if you could just speak to me.
Please, Mister Nkumbi. Just speak to me. Please say,
Mister Nkumbi, if you ever would, just one word.
I would be so grateful. So deeply grateful.
If I could hear, please. Just one word.
Mister Nkumbi?

(JULIUS *smiles. He places one hand on* BETSY's *shoulder. He nods. She holds his other hand.*)

(UDAYA DAWN *hears something. She goes to the patio upstage. She opens the door. She looks out.*)

(*A* GOAT *appears. And then a* LEOPARD. *They lie down together.*)

END OF PLAY

Playwright's Program Note, production at People's Light & Theatre Company, 2009

In early 2007, I decided to radically revise a script called *The Day of the Picnic*. This script had been presented at the O'Neill Center's 1983 National Playwrights Conference. It was produced at Yale Repertory Theatre in 1984 with James Earl Jones in the cast and at City Theatre Company. The play concerns, in part, a witch doctor's revenge on the widow of a white missionary thirty years later, but the original script completely skirted any real grappling with the subject of the British Colonial Government's suppression of the Mau Mau movement in Kenya in the 1950s. It also failed to deal with the redaction of the Hebrew Bible and New Testament canon, and the conflicting interpretations of these texts, which are germane to this particular drama. Beginning in 1990, I began to read extensively on these and other subjects and to take notes. Books that were important to me include: *Imperial Reckoning: The Untold Story of Britain's Gulag in Kenya* by Caroline Elkins; *History of the Hanged: The Dirty War in Kenya & the End of Empire* by David Anderson; books by Roland Oliver, Basil Davidson, Thomas Pakenham and Adam Hochschild; and numerous books by various ancient historians and Bible scholars, such as Peter Brown, Wayne Meeks, Margaret MacDonald, Carolyn Osiek, H.W.F. Saggs, Peter Heather. I completed in January, 2007 a first draft of what is fundamentally a new script. Characters were radically rewritten or simply replaced. A good 80% of the old dialogue was tossed. What remained was its original setting, its essential original story and the opening line with someone offstage calling out: "Yoo hoo!" This script was then further developed in rehearsed readings at New Dramatists in New York, the Playpenn Script Conference in Philadelphia and Playwrights Theatre of New Jersey, Madison, NJ. I am particularly grateful for the help of Emily Morse, Director of Artistic Development at New Dramatists, for her help as a dramatrug both at Playpenn and New Dramatists. I am grateful to be working in a field, such as theatre, where we can be allowed to stumble and fumble, and even take twenty-five years or so, before we might begin to perceive how the idea for a play might unfold.